I0020928

FORWARD/COMMENTARY

The National Institute of Standards and Technology (NIST) is a measurement standards laboratory, and a non-regulatory agency of the **United States Department of Commerce**. Its mission is to promote innovation and industrial competitiveness. Founded in 1901, as the National Bureau of Standards, NIST was formed with the mandate to provide standard weights and measures, and to serve as the national physical laboratory for the United States. With a world-class measurement and testing laboratory encompassing a wide range of areas of computer science, mathematics, statistics, and systems engineering, NIST's cybersecurity program supports its overall mission to promote U.S. innovation and industrial competitiveness by advancing measurement science, standards, and related technology through research and development in ways that enhance economic security and improve our quality of life.

The need for cybersecurity standards and best practices that address interoperability, usability and privacy has been shown to be critical for the nation. NIST's cybersecurity programs seek to enable greater development and application of practical, innovative security technologies and methodologies that enhance the country's ability to address current and future computer and information security challenges.

The cybersecurity publications produced by NIST cover a wide range of cybersecurity concepts that are carefully designed to work together to produce a holistic approach to cybersecurity primarily for government agencies and constitute the best practices used by industry. This holistic strategy to cybersecurity covers the gamut of security subjects from development of secure encryption standards for communication and storage of information while at rest to how best to recover from a cyber-attack.

Why buy a book you can download for free?   We print this so you don't have to.

Some are available only in electronic media. Some online docs are missing pages or barely legible.

We at 4th Watch Publishing are former government employees, so we know how government employees actually use the standards. When a new standard is released, an engineer prints it out, punches holes and puts it in a 3-ring binder. While this is not a big deal for a 5 or 10-page document, many NIST documents are over 100 pages and printing a large document is a time-consuming effort. So, an engineer that's paid $75 an hour is spending hours simply printing out the tools needed to do the job. That's time that could be better spent doing engineering. We publish these documents so engineers can focus on what they were hired to do – engineering. It's much more cost-effective to just order the latest version from Amazon.com

If there is a standard you would like published, let us know. Our web site is usgovpub.com

Many of our titles are available as ePubs for Kindle, iPad, Nook, remarkable, BOOX, and Sony eReaders.

Why buy an eBook when you can access data on a website for free? HYPERLINKS

Yes, many books are available as a PDF, but not all PDFs are bookmarked? Do you really want to search a 6,500-page PDF document manually? Load our copy onto your Kindle, PC, iPad, Android Tablet, Nook, or iPhone (download the FREE kindle App from the APP Store) and you have an easily searchable copy. Most devices will allow you to easily navigate an ePub to any Chapter. Note that there is a distinction between a Table of Contents and "Page Navigation". Page Navigation refers to a different sort of Table of Contents. Not one appearing as a page in the book, but one that shows up on the device itself when the reader accesses the navigation feature. Readers can click on a navigation link to jump to a Chapter or Subchapter. Once there, most devices allow you to "pinch and zoom" in or out to easily read the text. (Unfortunately, downloading the free sample file at Amazon.com does not include this feature. You have to buy a copy to get that functionality, but as inexpensive as eBooks are, it's worth it.) Kindle allows you to do word search and Page Flip (temporary place holder takes you back when you want to go back and check something). Visit **www.usgovpub.com** to learn more.

NIST Special Publication 800-177
Revision 1

Trustworthy Email

Scott Rose
J. Stephen Nightingale
Simson Garfinkel
Ramaswamy Chandramouli

This publication is available free of charge from:
https://doi.org/10.6028/NIST.SP.800-177r1

COMPUTER SECURITY

National Institute of
Standards and Technology
U.S. Department of Commerce

NIST Special Publication 800-177
Revision 1

Trustworthy Email

Scott Rose
J. Stephen Nightingale[*]
Advanced Network Technology Division
Information Technology Laboratory

Simson L. Garfinkel
US Census Bureau

Ramaswamy Chandramouli
Computer Security Division
Information Technology Laboratory

[*]*Former employee; all work for this publication was done while at NIST*

This publication is available free of charge from:
https://doi.org/10.6028/NIST.SP.800-177r1

February 2019

U.S. Department of Commerce
Wilbur L. Ross, Jr., Secretary

National Institute of Standards and Technology
Walter Copan, NIST Director and Under Secretary of Commerce for Standards and Technology

Authority

This publication has been developed by NIST in accordance with its statutory responsibilities under the Federal Information Security Modernization Act (FISMA) of 2014, 44 U.S.C. § 3551 *et seq.*, Public Law (P.L.) 113-283. NIST is responsible for developing information security standards and guidelines, including minimum requirements for federal information systems, but such standards and guidelines shall not apply to national security systems without the express approval of appropriate federal officials exercising policy authority over such systems. This guideline is consistent with the requirements of the Office of Management and Budget (OMB) Circular A-130, Section 8b(3), *Securing Agency Information Systems*, as analyzed in Circular A-130, Appendix IV: *Analysis of Key Sections*. Supplemental information is provided in Circular A-130, Appendix III, *Security of Federal Automated Information Resources*.

Nothing in this publication should be taken to contradict the standards and guidelines made mandatory and binding on federal agencies by the Secretary of Commerce under statutory authority. Nor should these guidelines be interpreted as altering or superseding the existing authorities of the Secretary of Commerce, Director of the OMB, or any other federal official. This publication may be used by nongovernmental organizations on a voluntary basis and is not subject to copyright in the United States. Attribution would, however, be appreciated by NIST.

National Institute of Standards and Technology Special Publication 800-177 Revision 1
Natl. Inst. Stand. Technol. Spec. Publ. 800-177 Revision 1, 128 pages (February 2019)
CODEN: NSPUE2

This publication is available free of charge from:
https://doi.org/10.6028/NIST.SP.800-177r1

Comments on this publication may be submitted to:

National Institute of Standards and Technology
Attn: Advanced Network Technologies Division, Information Technology Laboratory
100 Bureau Drive (Mail Stop 8920) Gaithersburg, MD 20899-8920
Email: SP800-177@nist.gov

All comments are subject to release under the Freedom of Information Act (FOIA).

Reports on Computer Systems Technology

The Information Technology Laboratory (ITL) at the National Institute of Standards and Technology (NIST) promotes the U.S. economy and public welfare by providing technical leadership for the Nation's measurement and standards infrastructure. ITL develops tests, test methods, reference data, proof of concept implementations, and technical analyses to advance the development and productive use of information technology. ITL's responsibilities include the development of management, administrative, technical, and physical standards and guidelines for the cost-effective security and privacy of other than national security-related information in federal information systems. The Special Publication 800-series reports on ITL's research, guidelines, and outreach efforts in information system security, and its collaborative activities with industry, government, and academic organizations.

Abstract

This document gives recommendations and guidelines for enhancing trust in email. The primary audience includes enterprise email administrators, information security specialists and network managers. This guideline applies to federal IT systems and will also be useful for small or medium sized organizations. Technologies recommended in support of core Simple Mail Transfer Protocol (SMTP) and the Domain Name System (DNS) include mechanisms for authenticating a sending domain: Sender Policy Framework (SPF), Domain Keys Identified Mail (DKIM) and Domain based Message Authentication, Reporting and Conformance (DMARC). Recommendations for email transmission security include Transport Layer Security (TLS) and associated certificate authentication protocols. Recommendations for email content security include the encryption and authentication of message content using S/MIME (Secure/Multipurpose Internet Mail Extensions) and associated certificate and key distribution protocols.

Keywords

Email; Simple Mail Transfer Protocol (SMTP); Transport Layer Security (TLS); Sender Policy Framework (SPF); Domain Keys Identified Mail (DKIM); Domain based Message Authentication, Reporting and Conformance (DMARC); Authentication of Named Entities (DANE); S/MIME; OpenPGP.

Audience

This document gives recommendations and guidelines for enhancing trust in email. The primary audience for these recommendations is federal enterprise email administrators, information security specialists and network managers. While some of the guidelines in this document pertain to federal IT systems and network policy, most of the document will be more general in nature and could apply to any organization.

For most of this document, it will be assumed that the organization has some or all responsibility for email and can configure or manage its own email and Domain Name System (DNS) systems. Even if this is not the case, the guidelines and recommendations in this document may help in education about email security and can be used to produce a set of requirements for a contracted service.

Trademark Information

All registered trademarks belong to their respective organizations.

Executive Summary

This document gives recommendations and guidelines for enhancing trust in email. The primary audience includes enterprise email administrators, information security specialists and network managers. This guideline applies to federal IT systems and will also be useful for small or medium sized organizations.

Email is a core application of computer networking and has been such since the early days of Internet development. In those early days, networking was a collegial, research-oriented enterprise. Security was not a consideration. The past forty years have seen diversity in applications deployed on the Internet, and worldwide adoption of email by research organizations, governments, militaries, businesses and individuals. At the same time there has been an associated increase in (Internet-based) criminal and nuisance threats.

The Internet's underlying core email protocol, Simple Mail Transport Protocol (SMTP), was first adopted in 1982 and is still deployed and operated today. However, this protocol is susceptible to a wide range of attacks including man-in-the-middle content modification and content surveillance. The basic standards have been modified and augmented over the years with adaptations that mitigate some of these threats. With spoofing protection, integrity protection, encryption and authentication, properly implemented email systems can be regarded as sufficiently secure for government, financial and medical communications.

NIST has been active in the development of email security guidelines for many years. The most recent NIST guideline on secure email is NIST SP 800-45, Version 2 of February 2007, *Guidelines on Electronic Mail Security*. The purpose of that document is:

> "To recommend security practices for designing, implementing and operating email systems on public and private networks,"

Those recommendations include practices for securing the environments around enterprise mail servers and mail clients, and efforts to eliminate server and workstation compromise. This guide complements SP 800-45 by providing more up-to-date recommendations and guidance for email digital signatures and encryption (via S/MIME), recommendations for protecting against unwanted email (spam), and recommendations concerning other aspects of email system deployment and configuration.

Following a description of the general email infrastructure and a threat analysis, these guidelines cluster into techniques for authenticating a sending domain, techniques for assuring email transmission security and those for assuring email content security. The bulk of the security enhancements to email rely on records and keys stored in the Domain Name System (DNS) by one party and extracted from there by the other party. Increased reliance on the DNS is permissible because of the recent security enhancements there, in particular the development and widespread deployment of the DNS Security Extensions (DNSSEC) to provide source authentication and integrity protection of DNS data.

The purpose of authenticating the sending domain is to guard against senders (both random and malicious actors) from spoofing another's domain and initiating messages with bogus content, and against malicious actors from modifying message contents in transit. Sender Policy Framework (SPF) is the standardized way for a sending domain to identify and assert the authorized mail senders for a given domain. Domain Keys Identified Mail (DKIM) is the mechanism for asserting sending servers and eliminating the vulnerability of man-in-the-middle content modification by using digital signatures generated from the sending mail server.

Domain based Message Authentication, Reporting and Conformance (DMARC) was conceived to allow email senders to specify policy on how their mail should be handled, the types of security reports that receivers can send back, and the frequency those reports should be sent. Standardized handling of SPF and DKIM removes guesswork about whether a given message is authentic, benefitting receivers by allowing more certainty in quarantining and rejecting unauthorized mail. In particular, receivers compare the "From" address in the message to the SPF and DKIM results, if present, and the DMARC policy in the DNS. The results are used to determine how the mail should be handled. The receiver sends reports to the domain owner about mail claiming to originate from their domain. These reports should illuminate the extent to which unauthorized users are using the domain, and the proportion of mail received that is "good."

Man-in-the-middle attacks can intercept cleartext email messages as they are transmitted hop-by-hop between mail relays. Any bad actor that can passively monitor network traffic can read such mail as it travels from submission to delivery systems. Email message confidentiality can be assured by encrypting traffic along the path. The Transport Layer Security Protocol (TLS) uses an encrypted channel to protect message transfers from man-in-the-middle attacks. TLS relies on the Public Key Infrastructure (PKI) system of X.509 certificates to carry exchange material and provide information about the entity holding the certificate. These are usually generated by a Certificate Authority (CA). The global CA ecosystem has in recent years become the subject to attack and has been successfully compromised more than once. One way to protect against CA compromises is to use the DNS to allow domains to specify their intended certificates or vendor CAs. Such uses of DNS require that the DNS itself be secured with DNSSEC. Correctly configured deployment of TLS may not stop a passive eavesdropper from viewing encrypted traffic but does practically eliminate the chance of deciphering it.

Server to server transport layer encryption also assures the integrity of email in transit, but senders and receivers who desire end-to-end assurance, (i.e., mailbox to mailbox) may wish to implement end-to-end, message-based authentication and confidentiality protections. The sender may wish to digitally sign and/or encrypt the message content, and the receiver can authenticate and/or decrypt the received message. Secure Multipurpose Internet Mail Extensions (S/MIME) is the recommended protocol for email end-to-end authentication and confidentiality. This usage of S/MIME is not common at the present time but is recommended. Certificate distribution remains a significant challenge when using S/MIME, especially the distribution of certificates between organizations. Research is underway on protocols that will allow the DNS to be used as a lightweight publication infrastructure for S/MIME certificates.

S/MIME is useful for authenticating email, since the protocol usually includes PKI certificates in messages in order to authenticate them, avoiding the necessity of distributing the sender's public key certificate in advance. Encrypted mass mailings are more problematic, as S/MIME senders need to possess the certificate of each recipient if the sender wishes to send encrypted mail.

Email communications cannot be made trustworthy with a single package or application. It involves incremental additions to basic subsystems, with each technology adapted to a particular task. Some of the techniques use other protocols such as DNS to facilitate specific security functions like domain authentication, content encryption and message originator authentication. These can be implemented discretely or in aggregate, according to organizational needs.

Table of Contents

List of Figures

List of Tables

1   Introduction

1.1   What This Guide Covers

This guide provides recommendations for deploying protocols and technologies that improve the trustworthiness of email. These recommendations reduce the risk of spoofed email being used as an attack vector and reduce the risk of email contents being disclosed to unauthorized parties. These recommendations cover both the email sender and receiver.

Several of the protocols discussed in this guide use technologies beyond the core email protocols and systems. These include the Domain Name System (DNS), Public Key Infrastructure (PKI) and other core Internet protocols. This guide discusses how these systems can be used to provide security services for email.

1.2   What This Guide Does Not Cover

This guide views email as a service, and thus it does not discuss topics such as individual server hardening, configuration and network planning. These topics are covered in NIST Special Publication 800-45, Version 2 of February 2007, *Guidelines on Electronic Mail Security* [SP800-45]. This guide should be viewed as a companion document to SP 800-45 that provides more updated guidance and recommendations that covers multiple components. This guide attempts to provide a holistic view of email and will only discuss individual system recommendations as examples warrant.

Likewise, this guide does not give specific configuration details for email components. There are a variety of hardware and software components that perform one or multiple email related tasks and it would be impossible to list them all in one guide. This guide will discuss protocols and configuration in an implementation neutral manner and administrators will need to consult their system documentation on how to execute the guidance for their specific implementations.

1.3   Document Structure

The rest of the document is presented in the following manner:

- **Section 2:** Discusses the core email protocols and the main components such as Mail Transfer Agents (MTA) and Mail User Agents (MUA), and cryptographic email formats.

- **Section 3:** Discusses the threats against an organization's email service such as phishing, spam and denial of service (DoS).

- **Section 4:** Discusses the protocols and techniques a sending domain can use to authenticate valid email senders for a given domain. This includes protocols such as Sender Policy Framework (SPF), DomainKeys Identified Mail (DKIM) and Domain-based Message and Reporting Conformance (DMARC).

- **Section 5:** Discusses server-to-server and end-to-end email authentication and confidentiality of message contents. This includes email sent over Transport Layer Security (TLS), Secure Multipurpose Internet Mail Extensions (S/MIME) and OpenPGP.

- **Section 6:** Discusses technologies to reduce unsolicited and (often) malicious email messages sent to a domain.

- **Section 7:** Discusses email security as it relates to end users and the final hop between local mail delivery servers and email clients. This includes Internet Message Access Protocol (IMAP), Post Office Protocol (POP3), and techniques for email encryption.

1.4 Conventions Used in this Guide

Throughout this guide, the following format conventions are used to denote special use text:

keyword - The text relates to a protocol keyword or text used as an example.

Security Recommendation: - Denotes a recommendation that administrators should note and account for when deploying the given protocol or security feature.

URLs are also included in the text and references to guide readers to a given website or online tool designed to aid administrators. This is not meant to be an endorsement of the website or any product/service offered by the website publisher. All URLs were considered valid at the time of writing.

2   Elements of Email

2.1   Email Components

There are a number of software components used to produce, send and transfer email. These components can be classified as clients or servers, although some components act as both. Some components are used interactively, and some are completely automated. In addition to the core components, some organizations use special purpose components that provide a specific set of security features. There are also other components used by mail servers when performing operations. These include the Domain Name System (DNS) and other network infrastructure pieces.

Fig 2-1 shows the relationship between the email system components on a network, which are described below in greater detail.

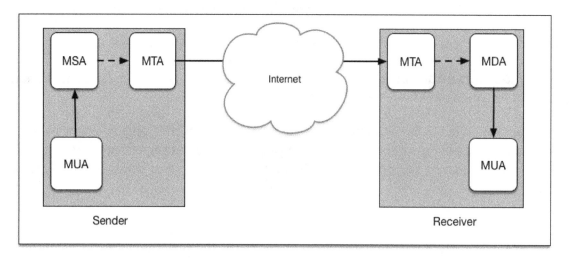

Figure 2-1: Main Components Used for Email

2.1.1   Mail User Agents (MUAs)

Most end users interact with their email system via a Mail User Agent (MUA). A MUA is a software component (or web interface) that allows an end user to compose and send messages and to one or more recipients. A MUA transmits new messages to a server for further processing (either final delivery or transfer to another server). The MUA is also the component used by end users to access a mailbox where in-bound emails have been delivered. MUAs are available for a variety of systems including mobile hosts. The proper secure configuration for a MUA depends on the MUA in question and the system it is running on. Some basic recommendations can be found in Section 7.

MUAs may utilize several protocols to connect to and communicate with email servers, (see Section 2.3.2 below). There may also be other features as well such as a cryptographic interface for producing encrypted and/or digitally signed email.

2.1.2 Mail Transfer Agents (MTAs)

Email is transmitted, in a "store and forward" fashion, across networks via Mail Transfer Agents (MTAs). MTAs communicate using the Simple Mail Transfer Protocol (SMTP) described below and act as both client and server, depending on the situation. For example, an MTA can act as a server when accepting an email message from an end user's MUA, then act as a client in connecting to and transferring the message to the recipient domain's MTA for final delivery.

MTAs can be described with more specialized language that denotes specific functions:

- **Mail Submission Agents (MSA):** An MTA that accepts mail from MUAs (usually after authenticating the sender) and begins the transmission process by sending it to a MTA for further processing. Often the MSA and first-hop MTA is the same process, just fulfilling both roles.

- **Mail Delivery Agent (MDA):** An MTA that receives mail from an organization's inbound MTA and ultimately places the message in a specific mailbox. Like the MSA, the MDA could be a combined in-bound MTA and MDA component.

Mail servers may also perform various security functions to prevent malicious email from being delivered or include authentication credentials such as digital signatures (see Sender Policy Framework Section 4.3 and DomainKeys Identified Mail (DKIM) Section 4.5). These security functions may be provided by other components that act as lightweight MTAs or these functions may be added to MTAs via filters or patches.

An email message may pass through multiple MTAs before reaching the final recipient. Each MTA in the chain may have its own security policy (which may be uniform within an organization but may not be uniform) and there is currently no way for a sender to request a particular level of security for the email message. However, there is work in progress[1] for specifying how a client can request the use of TLS for message transmission.

2.1.3 Special Use Components

In addition to MUAs and MTAs, an organization may use one or more special purpose components for a particular task. These components may provide a security function such as malware filtering or may provide some business process functionality such as email archiving or content filtering. These components may exchange messages with other parts of the email infrastructure using all or part of SMTP (see Section 2.3.1) or use another protocol altogether.

Given the variety of components, there is no one single set of configurations for an administrator to deploy, and different organizations have deployed very different email architectures. An

---

[1] J. Fenton. *SMTP Require TLS Option*. Work in Progress. https://datatracker.ietf.org/doc/draft-ietf-uta-smtp-require-tls/.

administrator should consult the documentation for their given component and their existing site-specific architecture.

2.1.4 Special Considerations for Cloud and Hosted Service Customers

Organizations that outsource their email service (whole or in part) may not have direct access to MTAs, Authoritative DNS servers, or any possible special use components. In cases of Email as a Service (EaaS), the service provider is responsible for the email infrastructure. Customers of Infrastructure as a Service (IaaS) may have sufficient access privileges to configure their email servers themselves. In either architecture, the enterprise may have complete configuration control over MUAs in use.

2.1.5 Email Server and Related Component Architecture

How an organization architects its email infrastructure is beyond the scope of this document. It is up to the organization and administrators to identify key requirements (availability, security, etc.) and available product or service offerings to meet those requirements. Federal IT administrators also need to take relevant federal IT policies into account when acquiring and deploying email systems.

Guidance for deploying and configuring an MTA for federal agency use exists as NIST SP 800-45 *Guidelines on Electronic Mail Security* [SP800-45]. In addition, the Dept. of Homeland Security (DHS) has produced the *Email Gateway Reference Architecture* [REFARCH] for agencies to use as a guide when setting up or modifying the email infrastructure for an agency.

2.2 Related Components

In addition to MUAs and MTAs, there are other network components used to support the email service for an organization. Most obviously is the physical infrastructure: the cables, wireless access points, routers and switches that make up the network. In addition, there are network components used by email components in the process of completing their tasks. This includes the DNS, Public Key Infrastructure (PKI), and network security components that are used by the organization.

2.2.1 Domain Name System (DNS)

The DNS is a global, distributed database and associated lookup protocol. DNS is used to map a piece of information (most commonly a domain name) to an IP address or some other network information used by a computer system. The DNS is used by MUAs to find MSAs and by MTAs to find the IP address of the next-hop server for mail delivery. Sending MTAs query DNS for the Mail Exchange Resource Record (MX RR) of the recipient's domain (the part of an email address to the right of the "@" symbol) in order to find the receiving MTA to contact.

In addition to the "forward" DNS (translate domain names to IP addresses or other data), there is also the "reverse" DNS tree that is used to map IP addresses to their corresponding DNS name, or other data. Traditionally, the reverse tree is used to obtain the domain name for a given client based on the source IP address of the connection, but it is also used as a crude, highly imperfect authentication check. A host compares the forward and reverse DNS trees to check that the remote connection is likely valid and not a potential attacker abusing a valid IP address block. This can be more problematic in IPv6, where even small networks can be assigned very large address blocks. Email anti-abuse consortiums such as the Messaging, Malware Mobile Anti-Abuse Working Group (M^3AAWG) recommend that enterprises should make sure that DNS reverse trees identify the authoritative mail servers for a domain [M3AAWG].

The DNS is also used as the publication method for protocols designed to protect email and combat malicious, spoofed email. Technologies such as SPF, DKIM and other use the DNS to publish policy artifacts or public keys that can be used by receiving MTAs to validate that a given message originated from the purported sending domain's mail servers. These protocols are discussed in Section 4. In addition, there are new proposals to encode end-user certificates or public keys (for S/MIME or OpenPGP) in the DNS using a mailbox as the hostname. These protocols are discussed in Section 5.3.

A third use of the DNS with email is with reputation services. These services provide information about the authenticity of an email based on the purported sending domain or originating IP address. These services do not rely on the anti-spoofing techniques described above but through historical monitoring, domain registration history, and other information sources. These services are often used to combat unsolicited bulk email (i.e., spam) and malicious email that could contain malware or links to subverted websites.

The Domain Name System Security Extensions (DNSSEC) [RFC4033] provides cryptographic security for DNS queries. Without security, DNS can be subjected to a variety of spoofing and man-in-the-middle attacks. Recommendations for deploying DNS in a secure manner are beyond the scope of this document. Readers are directed to NIST SP 800-81 [SP800-81] for recommendations on deploying DNSSEC.

2.2.2 Enterprise Perimeter Security Components

Organizations may utilize security components that do not directly handle email but may perform operations that affect email transactions. These include network components like firewalls, Intrusion Detection Systems (IDS) and similar malware scanners. These systems may not play any direct role in the sending and delivering of email but may have a significant impact if misconfigured. This could result in legitimate SMTP connections being denied and the failure of valid email to be delivered. Network administrators should take the presence of these systems into consideration when making changes to an organization's email infrastructure. This document makes no specific recommendations regarding these peripheral components.

2.2.3 Public Key Infrastructure (PKI)

Organizations that send and receive S/MIME or OpenPGP protected messages, as well as those that use TLS, will also need to rely on the certificate infrastructure (S/MIME) or key server ecosystem (OpenPGP) used with these protocols. These infrastructures do not always require the deployment of a dedicated system, but does require administrator time to obtain, configure and distribute security credentials to end-users.

X.509 certificates can be used to authenticate one (or both) ends of a TLS connection when SMTP runs over TLS (usually MUA to MTA). S/MIME also uses X.509 certificates [RFC5280] to certify and store public keys used to validate digital signatures and encrypt email. The Internet X.509 Public Key Infrastructure Certificate and Certificate Revocation List (CRL) Profile is commonly called PKIX and is specified by [RFC5280]. Certificate Authorities (CA) (or the organization itself) issues X.509 certificates for an individual end-user or enterprise/business role (performed by a person or not) that sends email (for S/MIME). Recommendations for S/MIME protected email are given in Section 5. Recommendations for SMTP over TLS are given in Section 5. Federal agency network administrators should also consult NIST SP 800-57 Part 3 [SP800-57P3] and the Federal PKI Key Recovery Policy [FPKIKRP] for further guidance on cryptographic parameters and deployment of any PKI components and credentials within an organization.

2.3 Email protocols

There are two types of protocols used in the transmission of email. The first are the protocols used to transfer messages between MTAs and their end users (using MUAs). The second is the protocol used to transfer messages between mail servers.

This guide is not meant to be an in-depth discussion of the protocols used in email. These protocols are discussed here simply for background information.

2.3.1 Simple Mail Transfer Protocol (SMTP)

Email messages are transferred from one mail server to another (or from an MUA to MSA/MTA) using SMTP. SMTP was originally specified in 1982 in [RFC821] and has undergone several revisions, the most current being [RFC5321]. SMTP is a text-based client-server protocol where the client (email sender) contacts the server (next-hop MTA) and issues a set of commands to tell the server about the message to be sent, and then transmits the message itself. The majority of these commands are ASCII text messages sent by the client and a resulting return code (also ASCII text) returned by the server. The basic SMTP connection procedure is shown below in Figure 2-2:

> **Client connects to port 25**
> Server: 220 mx.example.com
> **Client: HELO mta.example.net**
> *S: 250 Hello mta.example.net, I am glad to meet you*
> **C: MAIL FROM:<alice@example.org>**
> S: 250 Ok
> **C: RCPT TO:<bob@example.com>**
> S: 354 End data with <CR><LF>.<CR><LF>
> *Client sends message headers and body*
> **C: .**
> S: 250 Ok: queued as 12345
> **C: QUIT**
> S: 221 Bye
> *Server closes the connection*

Figure 2-2: Basic SMTP Connection Set-up

In the above, the client initiates the connection using TCP over port 25[2]. After the initial connection, the client and server perform a series of SMTP transactions to send the message. These transactions take the form of first stating the return address of the message (known as the return path) using the **MAIL** command, then the recipient(s) using the **RCPT** command and ending with the **DATA** command which contains the header and body of the email message. After each command the server responds with either a positive or negative (i.e., error) code.

SMTP servers can advertise the availability of options during the initial connection. These extensions are currently defined in [RFC5321]. These options usually deal with the transfer of the actual message and will not be covered in this guide except for the STARTTLS option. This option advertised by the server is used to indicate to the client that Transport Layer Security (TLS) is available. SMTP over TLS allows the email message to be sent over an encrypted channel to protect against monitoring a message in transit. Recommendations for configuring SMTP over TLS are given in Section 5.2.

2.3.2 Mail Access Protocols (POP3, IMAP, MAPI/RPC)

MUAs typically do not use SMTP when retrieving mail from an end-user's mailbox, only for submission. MUAs use another client-server protocol to retrieve the mail from a server for display on an end-user's host system. These protocols are commonly called Mail Access Protocols and are either Post Office Protocol (POP) or Internet Message Access Protocol (IMAP). Most modern MUAs support both protocols but an enterprise service may restrict the use of one in favor of a single protocol for ease of administration or other reasons. Recommendations for the secure configuration of these protocols are given in Section 7.

---

[2] Although MUAs often use TCP port 587 when submitting email to be sent.

POP version 3 (POP3) [STD35] is the simpler of the two protocols and typically downloads all mail for a user from the server, then deletes the copy on the server, although there is an option to maintain it on the server. POP3 is similar to SMTP, in that the client connects to a port (normally port 110 or port 995 when using TLS) and sends ASCII commands, to which the server responds, only instead of sending messages, it retrieves messages from the MTA. When the session is complete, the client terminates the connection. POP3 transactions are normally done in the clear, but an extension is available to do POP3 over TLS using the STLS command, which is very similar to the STARTTLS option in SMTP. Clients may connect initially over port 110 and invoke the STLS command, or alternatively, most servers allow TLS by default connections on port 995.

IMAP [RFC3501] is an alternative to POP3 but includes more built-in features that make it more appealing for enterprise use. IMAP clients can download email messages, but the messages remain on the server. This and the fact that multiple clients can access the same mailbox simultaneously mean that end-users with multiple devices (laptop and smartphone for example), can keep their email synchronized across multiple devices. Like POP3, IMAP also has the ability to secure the connection between a client and a server. Traditionally, IMAP uses port 143 with no encryption. Encrypted IMAP runs over port 993, although modern IMAP servers also support the STARTTLS option on port 143.

In addition to POP3 and IMAP, there are other proprietary protocols in use with certain enterprise email implementations. Microsoft Exchange clients[3] can use the Messaging Application Programming Interface (MAPI/RPC) to access a mailbox on a Microsoft Exchange server (and some other compatible implementations). Some cloud providers require clients to access their cloud-based mailbox using a web portal as the MUA instead of a dedicated email client. With the exception of Microsoft's Outlook Web Access, most web portals use IMAP to access the user's mailbox.

2.3.3 Internet Email Addresses

Two distinct email addresses are used when sending an email via SMTP: the SMTP MAIL FROM address and the email header FROM address. The SMTP envelope MAIL FROM (also sometimes referred to as the *RFC5321.From*, or the *return-path* address, or *envelope From:*) is from address used in the client SMTP **mail from:** command as shown in Fig. 2-2 above. This email address may be altered by a sending MTA and may not always match the email address of the original sender. In the rest of this document, the term *envelope-From:* will be used. The second is the sender email address (sometimes referred to as the *RFC5322.From*). This is the address end-users see in the message header. In the rest of this document, the term *message-From:* will be used to denote this email address. The full details of the syntax and semantics of email addresses are defined in [RFC3696], [RFC5321] and [RFC5322].

---

[3] Administrators should consult their implementation's version-specific documentation on the correct security configuration.

Both types of contemporary email addresses consist of a local-part separated from a domain-part (a fully-qualified domain name) by an at-sign ("@") (e.g., **local-part@domain-part**). Typically, the local-part identifies a user of the mail system or server identified by the domain-part. The semantics of the local-part are not standardized, which occasionally causes confusion among both users and developers.[4] The domain-part is typically a fully qualified domain name of the system or service that hosts the user account that is identified by the local-part (e.g., **user@example.com**).

While the **user@example.com** is by far the most widely used form of email address, other forms of addresses are sometimes used. For example, the local-part may include "sub-addressing" that typically specifies a specific mailbox/folder within a user account (e.g., **user+folder@example.com**). Exactly how such local-parts are interpreted can vary across specific mail system implementations. The domain-part can refer to a specific MTA server, the domain of a specific enterprise or email service provider (ESP).

The remainder of this document will use the terms *email-address, local-part* and *domain-part* to refer the Internet email addresses and their component parts.

2.4   Email Formats

Email messages may be formatted as plain text or as compound documents containing one or more components and attachments. Modern email systems layer security mechanisms on top of these underlying systems.

2.4.1   Email Message Format: Multi-Purpose Internet Mail Extensions (MIME)

Internet email was originally sent as plain text ASCII messages [RFC2822]. The Multi-purpose Internet Mail Extensions (MIME) [RFC2045] [RFC2046] [RFC2047] allows email to contain non-ASCII character sets as well as other non-text message components and attachments. Essentially MIME allows for an email message to be broken into parts, with each part identified by a content type. Typical content types include **text/plain** (for ASCII text), **image/jpeg**, **text/html**, etc. A mail message may contain multiple parts, which themselves may contain multiple parts, allowing MIME-formatted messages to be included as attachments in other MIME-formatted messages. The available types are listed in an IANA registry[5] for developers, but not all may be understood by all MUAs.

2.4.2   Security in MIME Messages (S/MIME)

The Secure Multi-purpose Internet Mail Extensions (S/MIME) is a set of widely implemented proposed Internet standards for cryptographically securing email [RFC5750] [RFC5751]. S/MIME provides authentication, integrity and non-repudiation (via digital signatures) and confidentiality (via encryption). S/MIME utilizes asymmetric keys for cryptography (i.e., public

---

[4] For example, on some systems the local-parts local-part, lo.cal-part, and local-part+special represent the same mailbox or users, while on other systems they are different.

[5] http://www.iana.org/assignments/media-types/media-types.xhtml

key cryptography) where the public portion is normally encoded and presented as X.509 digital certificates.

With S/MIME, signing digital signatures and message encryption are two distinct operations: messages can be digitally signed, encrypted, or both digitally signed *and* encrypted (Figure 2-5). Because the process is first to sign and then encrypt, S/MIME is vulnerable to re-encryption attacks[6]; a protection is to include the name of the intended recipient in the encrypted message.

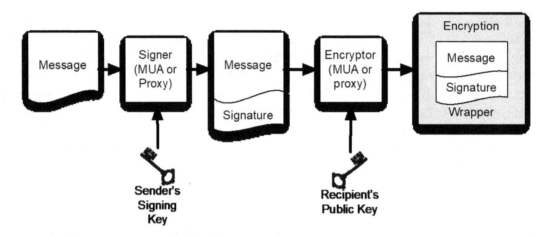

Figure 2-3: S/MIME Messages can be signed, encrypted, or both signed and encrypted

2.4.3   Pretty Good Privacy (PGP/OpenPGP)

OpenPGP [RFC3156] [RFC4880] is an alternative proposed Internet standard for digitally signing and encrypting email. OpenPGP is an adaptation of the message format implemented by the Pretty Good Privacy (PGP) email encryption system that was first released in 1991. Whereas the PGP formats were never formally specified, OpenPGP specifies open, royalty-free formats for encryption keys, signatures, and messages. Today the most widely used implementation of OpenPGP is Gnu Privacy Guard (gpg)[7], an open source command-line program that runs on many platforms, with APIs in popular languages such as C, Python and Perl. Most desktop and web-based applications that allow users to send and receive OpenPGP-encrypted mail rely on gpg as the actual cryptographic engine.

OpenPGP provides similar functionality as S/MIME, with three significant differences:

- **Key Certification:** Whereas X.509 certificates are issued by Certificate Authorities (or local agencies that have been delegated authority by a CA to issue certificates), users generate their own OpenPGP public and private keys and then solicit signatures for their public keys from individuals or organizations to which they are known. Whereas X.509 certificates can be signed by a single party, OpenPGP public keys can be signed by any

---

[6] Don Davis. 2001. Defective Sign & Encrypt in S/MIME, PKCS#7, MOSS, PEM, PGP, and XML. In *Proceedings of the General Track: 2001 USENIX Annual Technical Conference*, Yoonho Park (Ed.). USENIX Association, Berkeley, CA, USA, 65-78.

[7] https://www.gnupg.org/

number of parties. Whereas X.509 certificates are trusted if there is a valid PKIX chain to a trusted root, an OpenPGP public key is trusted if it is signed by another OpenPGP public key that is trusted by the recipient. This is called the "Web-of-Trust."

- **Key Distribution:** OpenPGP does not always include the sender's public key with each message, so it may be necessary for recipients of OpenPGP-messages to separately obtain the sender's public key in order to verify the message or respond to the sender with an encrypted message. Many organizations post OpenPGP keys on SSL-protected websites; people who wish to verify digital signatures or send these organizations encrypted mail need to manually download these keys and add them to their OpenPGP clients. Essentially this approach exploits the X.509 certificate infrastructure to certify OpenPGP keys, albeit with a process that requires manual downloading and verification.

  OpenPGP keys may also be registered with the OpenPGP "public key servers" (described below). OpenPGP "public key servers" are internet connected systems that maintain a database of PGP public keys organized by email address. Anyone may post a public key to the OpenPGP key servers, and that public key may contain any email address. Some OpenPGP clients can search the key servers for all of the keys that belong to a given email address and download the keys that match. Because there are no access controls on the servers, attackers are free to submit a fraudulent public key, and it is the responsibility of the person or program that downloads the public key to validate it.

- **Key and Certificate Revocation:** S/MIME keys are revoked using the PKIX revocation infrastructure of Certificate Revocation Lists [RFC5280] and the Online Certificate Status Protocol (OCSP) [RFC6960]. These protocols allow a certificate to be revoked at any time by the CA. With OpenPGP, in contrast a key is only allowed to be revoked by the key holder, and only with a Key Revocation Certificate. Thus, an OpenPGP user who loses access to a private key has no way to revoke the key if a Key Revocation Certificate was not prepared in advance. If a Key Revocation Certificate does exist, the certificate can be uploaded to a PGP Key Server, OpenPGP key servers are *generally not checked* by a client that already has a copy of an OpenPGP key. Thus, is it not clear how relying parties learn that an OpenPGP key has been revoked.

The Web-of-Trust is designed to minimize the problems of the key server. After an OpenPGP user downloads *all* of the keys associated with a particular email address, the correct OpenPGP certificate is selected by the signatures that it carries. Because Web-of-Trust supports arbitrary validation geometries, it allows both the top-down certification geometry of X.509 as well as peer-to-peer approaches. However, studies have demonstrated that users find this process confusing [WHITTEN1999], and the Web-of-Trust has not seen widespread adoption.

An alternative way to publish OpenPGP keys using the DNS is described in Section 5.3.2, OpenPGP, although the technique has not yet been widely adopted.

Like S/MIME, among the biggest hurdles of deploying OpenPGP are the need for users to create certificates in advance, the difficulty of obtaining the certificate of another user in order to send an encrypted message and incorporating this seamlessly into mail clients. However, in OpenPGP this difficulty impacts both digital signatures and encryption, since OpenPGP messages may not include the sender's public key (or generated certificate).

These differences are summarized in Table 2-1.

Table 2-1: Comparison of S/MIME and OpenPGP operations

Action	S/MIME	OpenPGP
Key creation	Users obtain X.509 certificates from employer (e.g., a US Government PIV card [FIPS 201]) or a Certificate Authority	Users make their own public/private key pairs and have them certified by associates.
Certificate Verification	PKIX: Certificates are verified using trusted roots that are installed on the end user's computer.	Web-of-Trust: Keys can be signed by any number of certifiers. Users base their trust decisions on whether or not they "trust" the keys that were used to sign the key.
Certificate Revocation	Certificates can be revoked by the CA or Issuer. Methods exist to publish revoked status of key (e.g., Certificate Revocation List, etc.).	Keys/Certificates can only be revoked by the public key's owner. Few options to signal key revocation and no uniform way for clients to see that a key has been revoked.
Obtaining public keys	Querying an LDAP server or exchanging digitally signed email messages.	PGP public key server or out-of-band mechanisms (e.g., posting a public key on a web page.)

2.5 Secure Web-Mail Solutions

Whereas S/MIME and OpenPGP provide a security overlay for traditional Internet email, some organizations have adopted secure web-mail systems as an alternative approach for sending encrypted e-mail messages between users. Secure web-mail systems can protect email messages solely with host-based security, or they can implement a cryptographic layer using S/MIME, OpenPGP, or other algorithms, such as the Boneh-Franklin (BF) and Boneh-Boyen (BB1) Identity-Based Encryption (IBE) algorithms [RFC5091] [RFC5408] [RFC5409].

Secure webmail systems can perform message decryption at the web server or on the end-user's client. In general, these systems are less secure than end-to-end systems because the private key is under the control of the web server, which also has access to the encrypted message. These systems cannot ensure non-repudiation since the server has direct access to the signing key.

An exception is webmail-based systems that employ client-side software to make use of a private key stored at the client—for example, a webmail plug-in that allows the web browser to make use of a private key stored in a FIPS-201 compliant smartcard. In these cases, the message is decrypted and displayed at the client, and the server does not access the decrypted text of the message.

3   Security Threats to an Email Service

The security threats to email service discussed in this section are related to canonical functions of the service such as: message submission (at the sender end), message transmission (transfer) and message delivery (at the recipient end).

Threats to the core email infrastructure functions can be classified as follows:

- **Integrity-related threats to the email system,** which could result in unauthorized access to an enterprises' email system, or spoofed email used to initiate an attack.
- **Confidentiality-related threats to email,** which could result in unauthorized disclosure of sensitive information.
- **Availability-related threats to the email system**, which could prevent end users from being able to send or receive email.

The security threats due to insufficiency of core security functions are not covered. These include threats to support infrastructure such as network components and firewalls, host OS and system threats, and potential attacks due to lax security policy at the end user or administrator level (e.g., poor password choices). Threats directed to these components and recommendations for enterprise security policies are found in other documents.

3.1   Integrity-related Threats

Integrity in the context of an email service assumes multiple dimensions. Each dimension can be the source of one or more integrity-related threats:

- Unauthorized email senders within an organization's IP address block
- Unauthorized email receivers within an organization's IP address block
- Unauthorized email messages from a valid DNS domain
- Tampering/Modification of email content from a valid DNS domain
- DNS Cache Poisoning
- Phishing and spear phishing

3.1.1   Unauthorized Email Senders within an Organization's IP Address Block

An unauthorized email sender is some MSA or MTA that sends email messages that appear to be from a user in a specific domain (e.g., **user@example.com**) but is not identified as a legitimate mail sender by the organization that runs the domain.

The main risk that an unauthorized email sender may pose to an enterprise is that a sender may be sending malicious email and using the enterprise's IP address block and reputation to avoid anti-spam filters. A related risk is that the sender may be sending emails that present themselves as legitimate communications from the enterprise itself.

There are many scenarios that might result in an unauthorized email sender:

- Malware present on an employee's laptop may be sending out email without the employee's knowledge.
- An employee (or intruder) may configure and operate a mail server without authorization.
- A device such as a photocopier or an embedded system may contain a mail sender that is attempting to send mail without anyone's knowledge.

One way to mitigate the risk of unauthorized senders is for the enterprise to block outbound port 25 (used by SMTP) for all hosts except those authorized to send mail. In addition, domains can deploy the sender authentication mechanism described in Section 4.3 (Sender Policy Framework (SPF)), using which senders can assert the IP addresses of the authorized MTAs for their domain using a DNS Resource Record.

Security Recommendation 3-1: To mitigate the risk of unauthorized sender, an enterprise administrator should block outbound port 25 (except for authorized mail senders) and look to deploy firewall or intrusion detection systems (IDS) that can alert the administrator when an unauthorized host is sending mail via SMTP to the Internet.

The proliferation of virtualization greatly increases the risk that an unauthorized virtual server running on a virtual machine (VM) within a particular enterprise might send email. This is because VMs may be configured (by default or otherwise) to run email servers (MTAs), and many VM hypervisors use network address translation (NAT) to share a single IP address between multiple VMs. Thus, a VM that is unauthorized to send email may share an IP address with a legitimate email sender. To prevent such a situation, ensure that VMs that are authorized mail senders and those VMs that are not authorized, do not share the same set of outbound IP addresses. An easy way to do this is assigning these VMs to different NAT instances. Alternatively, internal firewall rules can be used to block outbound port 25 for VMs that are not authorized to send outbound email.

Security Recommendation 3-2: Systems that are not involved in the organization's email infrastructure should be configured to not run Mail Transfer Agents (MTAs). Internal systems that need to send mail should be configured to use a trusted internal MSA.

3.1.2 Unauthorized Email Receiver within an Organization's IP Address Block

Unauthorized mail receivers are a risk to the enterprise IT security posture because they may be an entry point for malicious email. If the enterprise email administrator does not know of the unauthorized email receiver, they cannot guarantee the server is secure and provide the appropriate mail handling rules for the enterprise such as scanning for malicious links/code, filtering spam, etc. This could allow malware to bypass the enterprise perimeter defenses and enter the local network undetected.

Security Recommendation 3-3: To mitigate the risk of unauthorized receivers, an enterprise administrator should block inbound port 25 and look to deploy firewall or intrusion detection systems (IDS) that can alert the administrator when an unauthorized host is accepting mail via SMTP from the Internet.

3.1.3   Unauthorized Email Messages from a Valid DNS Domain (Address Spoofing)

Just as organizations face the risk of unauthorized email senders, they also face the risk that they might receive email from an unauthorized sender. This is sometimes called "spoofing," especially when one group or individual sends mail that appears to come from another. In a spoofing attack, the adversary spoofs messages using another (sometimes even non-existent) user's email address.

For example, an attacker sends emails that purport to come from **user@example.com**, when in fact the email messages are being sent from a compromised home router. Spoofing the message-From: address is trivial, as the SMTP protocol [RFC2821] allows clients to set any message-From: address. Alternatively, the adversary can simply configure a MUA with the name and email address of the spoofed user and send emails to an open SMTP relay (see [RFC2505] for a discussion of open relays).

The same malicious configuration activity can be used to configure and use wrong, misleading or malicious display names. When a display name that creates a degree of trust such as "Administrator" shows up on the email received at the recipient's end, it might make the recipient reveal some sensitive information which the recipient would not normally do. Thus, the spoofing threat/attack also has a social engineering dimension as well.

Section 4 discusses a variety of countermeasures for this type of threat. The first line of defense is to deploy domain-based authentication mechanisms (see Section 4). These mechanisms can be used to alert on or block email that was sent using a spoofed domain. Another end-to-end authentication technique is to use digital signatures to provide integrity protection for email headers. The digital signature used should cover the header portion of the email message that contains the address of the sender.

3.1.4   Tampering/Modification of Email Content

The content of an email message, just like any other message content traveling over the Internet, is liable to be altered in transit. Hence the content of the received email may not be the same as what the sender originally composed. The countermeasure for this threat is for the sender to digitally sign the message, attach the signature to the plaintext message and for the receiver to verify the signature.

There are several solutions available to mitigate this risk by either encrypting the transmission of email messages between servers using Transport Layer Security (TLS) for SMTP or using an end-to-end solution to digitally sign email between initial sender and final receiver. Recommendations for using TLS with SMTP are discussed in Section 5.2.1 and end-to-end email encryption protocols are discussed in Section 4.6. The use of digital signatures within the S/MIME and OpenPGP protocols is described in section 5.3.

3.1.5   DNS Cache Poisoning

Email systems rely on DNS for many functions. Some of them are:

- The sending MTA uses the DNS to find the IP address of the next-hop email server (assuming the To: address is not a local mailbox).
- The recipient email server (if domain-based email authentication is supported) uses the DNS to look for appropriate records in the sending DNS domain either to authenticate the sending email server (using SPF) or to authenticate an email message for its origin domain (using DKIM). See Section 5 for domain-based authentication mechanisms.

There are risks to using the DNS as a publication mechanism for authenticating email. First, those highly motivated to conduct phishing/spam campaigns, may attempt to spoof a given domain's DNS-based email authentication mechanisms in order to continue to deliver spoofed email masquerading as the domain in question. The second risk is that an attacker would spoof a domain's DNS-based authentication mechanisms in order to disrupt legitimate email from the source domain. For example, maliciously spoofing the SPF record of authorized mail relays, to exclude the domains legitimate MTAs, could result in all legitimate email from the target domain being dropped by other MTAs. Lastly, a resolver whose cache has been poisoned can potentially return the IP address desired by an attacker, rather than the legitimate IP address of a queried domain name. In theory, this allows email messages to be redirected or intercepted.

Another impact of a DNS server with a poisoned cache as well as a compromised web server is that the users are redirected to a malicious server/address when attempting to visit a legitimate web site. Although the visit to an illegitimate web site can occur by clicking on a link in a received email, this use case has no direct relevance to integrity of an email service and hence is outside the scope of this document.

As far as DNS cache poisoning is concerned, DNSSEC security extension [RFC4033] [RFC4034] [RFC4035] can provide protection from these kinds of attacks since it ensures the integrity of DNS resolution through an authentication chain from the root to the target domain of the original DNS query. However, even the presence of a single non-DNSSEC aware server in the chain can lead to a risk of compromise of the integrity of the DNS resolution.

3.1.6   Phishing and Spear Phishing

Phishing is the process of using a spoofed email to collect private information, distribute malware, or commit fraud. This is done with the intention of committing identity theft, gaining access to credit cards and bank accounts of the victim etc. Adversaries use a variety of tactics to make the recipient of the email believe that they have received the phishing email from a legitimate user or a legitimate domain, including:

- Using a message-From: address that looks very close to one of the legitimate addresses the user is familiar with or from someone claiming to be an authority (IT administrator, manager, etc.). Or altering the display name (also known as the friendly name).

- Using the email's content to present to the recipient an alarm, a financial lure, or otherwise attractive situation, that either makes the recipient panic or tempts the recipient into taking an action or providing requested information.
- Sending the email from an email using a legitimate account holder's software or credentials, typically using a bot that has taken control of the email client or malware that has stolen the user's credentials (described in detail in Section 3.3.1 below)

As part of the email message, the recipient may usually be asked to click on a link to what appears like a legitimate website, but in fact is a URL that will take the recipient into a spoofed website set up by the adversary. If the recipient clicks on the embedded URL, the victim often finds that the sign-in page, logos and graphics are identical to the legitimate website in the adversary-controlled website, thereby creating the trust necessary to make the recipient submit the required information such as user ID and the password. Some attackers use web pages to deliver malware directly to the victim's web browser.

In many instances, the phishing emails are generated in thousands without focus on profile of the victims. Hence, they will have a generic greeting such as "Dear Member", "Dear Customer" etc. A variant of phishing is *spear phishing* where the adversary is aware of, and specific about, the victim's profile. More than a generic phishing email, a spear phishing email makes use of more contextual information to make users believe that they are interacting with a legitimate source. For example, a spear phishing email may appear to relate to some specific item of personal importance or a relevant matter at the organization—for instance, discussing payroll discrepancies or a legal matter. As in phishing, the ultimate motive is the same—to lure the recipient to an adversary-controlled website masquerading as a legitimate website to collect sensitive information about the victim or attack the victim's computer.

There are two minor variations of phishing: *clone phishing* and *whaling*. Clone phishing is the process of cloning an email from a legitimate user carrying an attachment or link and then replacing the link or attachment alone with a malicious version and then sending altered email from an email address spoofed to appear to come from the original sender (carrying the pretext of re-sending or sending an updated version). Whaling is a type of phishing specifically targeted against high profile targets so that the resulting damage carries more publicity and/or financial rewards for the perpetrator is greater.

The most common countermeasures used against phishing are domain-based checks such as SPF, DKIM and DMARC (see Section 4). More elaborate is to design anti-phishing filters that can detect text commonly used in phishing emails, recovering hidden text in images, intelligent word recognition – detecting cursive, hand-written, rotated or distorted texts as well as the ability to detect texts on colored backgrounds. While these techniques will not prevent malicious email sent using compromised legitimate accounts, they can be used to reduce malicious email sent from spoofed domains or spoofed "From:" addresses.

3.2   Confidentiality-related Threats

A confidentiality-related threat occurs when the data stream containing email messages with sensitive information are accessible to an adversary. The type of attack that underlies this threat can be passive since the adversary only requires read access but not write access to the email data being transmitted. The two variations of this type of attack include:

- The adversary may have access to the packets that make up the email message as they move over a network. This access may come in the form of a passive wiretapping or eavesdropping attack.
- Software may be installed on a MTA that makes copies of email messages and delivers them to the adversary. For example, the adversary may have modified the target's email account so that a copy of every received message is forwarded to an email address outside the organization.
- The valid receiver's mail servers may be spoofed (or DNS MX reply spoofed), to get the sender to connect to a MTA controlled by an attacker.

Encryption is the best defense against eavesdropping attacks. Encrypting the email messages either between MTAs (using TLS as described in Section 5) can thwart attacks involving packet interception. End-to-end encryption (described in Section 5.3) can protect against both eavesdropping attacks as well as MTA software compromise.

A second form of passive attack is a traffic analysis attack. In this scenario, the adversary is not able to directly interpret the contents of an email message, mostly due to the fact that the message is encrypted. However, since inference of information is still possible in certain circumstances (depending upon interaction or transaction context) from the observation of external traffic characteristics (volume and frequency of traffic between any two entities) and hence the occurrence of this type of attack constitutes a confidentiality threat.

Although the impact of traffic analysis is limited in scope, it is much easier to perform this attack in practice—especially if part of the email transmission media uses a wireless network, if packets are sent over a shared network, or if the adversary has the ability to run network management or monitoring tools against the victim's network. TLS encryption provides some protection against traffic analysis attacks, as the attacker is prevented from seeing any message headers. End-to-end email encryption protocols do not protect message headers, as the headers are needed for delivery to the destination mailbox. Thus, organizations may wish to employ both kinds of encryption to secure email from confidentiality threats.

3.3   Availability-related Threats

An availability threat exists in the email infrastructure (or for that matter any IT infrastructure), when potential events occur that prevent the resources of the infrastructure from functioning according to their intended purpose. The following availability-related threats exist in an email infrastructure:

- Email Bombing,
- Unsolicited Bulk Email (UBE) – also called "Spam," and

- Availability of email servers.

3.3.1 Email Bombing

Email bombing is a type of attack that involves sending several thousands of messages to a particular mailbox in order to cause overflow. These can be many large messages or a very large number of small messages. Such a mailbox will become unusable for the legitimate email account holder to access. No new messages can be delivered, and the sender receives an error asking to resend the message. In some instances, the mail server may also crash.

The motive for email bombing is denial of service (DoS). A DoS attack by definition either prevents authorized access to resources or causes delay (e.g., long response times) of time-critical operations. Hence email bombing is a major availability threat to an email system since it can potentially consume substantial Internet bandwidth as well as storage space in the message stores of recipients. An email bombing attack can be launched in several ways.

There are many ways to perpetrate an email bombing attack, including:

- An adversary can employ any (anonymous) email account to constantly bombard the victim's email account with arbitrary messages (that may contain very long large attachments).
- If an adversary controls an MTA, the adversary can run a program that automatically composes and transmits messages.
- An adversary can post a controversial or significant official statement to a large audience (e.g., a social network) using the victim's return email address. Humans will read the message and respond with individually crafted messages that may be very hard to filter with automated techniques. The responses to this posting will eventually flood the victim's email account.
- An adversary may subscribe the victim's email address to many mailing lists ("listservers"). The generated messages are then sent to the victim, until the victim's email address is unsubscribed from those lists.

Possible countermeasures for protection against email bombing are: (a) Use filters that are based on the logic of filtering identical messages that are received within a chosen short span of time and (b) configuring email receivers to block messages beyond a certain size and/or containing attachments that exceed a certain size.

3.3.2 Unsolicited Bulk Email (Spam)

Spam is the internet slang for unsolicited bulk email (UBE). Spam refers to indiscriminately sent messages that are unsolicited, unwanted, irrelevant and/or inappropriate, such as commercial advertising in mass quantities. Thus spam, generally, is not targeted towards a particular email receiver or domain. However, when the volume of spam coming into a particular email domain exceeds a certain threshold, it has availability implications since it results in increased network traffic and storage space for message stores. Spam that looks for random gullible victims or targets particular users or groups of users with malicious intent (gathering sensitive information for physical harm or for committing financial fraud) is called phishing. From the above discussion of email bombing attacks, it should be clear that spam can sometimes be a type of email bombing.

Protecting the email infrastructure against spam is a challenging problem. This is due to the fact that the two types of techniques currently used to combat spam have limitations. See Section 6 for a more detailed discussion of unsolicited bulk email.

3.3.3 Availability of Email Servers

The email infrastructure, just like any other IT infrastructure, should provide for fault tolerance and avoid single points of failure. A domain with only a single email server or a domain with multiple email servers, but all located in a single IP subnet is likely to encounter availability problems either due to software glitches in MTA, hardware maintenance issues or local data center network problems. The typical measures for ensuring high availability of email as a service are: (a) Multiple MTAs with placement based on the email traffic load encountered by the enterprise; and, (b) Distribution of email servers in different network segments or even physical locations.

3.4 Summary of Threats and Mitigations

A summary of the email related threats to an enterprise is given in Table 3-1. This includes threats to both the email the receiver and the purported sender - often spoofed, and who may not be aware an email was sent using their domain. Mitigations are listed in the final column to reduce the risk of the attack being successful, or to prevent them.

Table 3-1 Email-based Threats and Mitigations

Threat	Impact on Purported Sender	Impact on Receiver	Mitigation
Email sent by unauthorized MTA in enterprise (e.g., malware botnet).	Loss of reputation, valid email from enterprise may be blocked as possible spam/phishing attack.	UBE and/or email containing malicious links or attachments may be delivered into user inboxes.	Deployment of domain-based authentication techniques (see Section 4). Use of digital signatures over email (see Section 6). Blocking outbound port 25 for all non-mail sending hosts.

Threat	Impact on Purported Sender	Impact on Receiver	Mitigation
Email message sent using spoofed or unregistered sending domain.	Loss of reputation, valid email from enterprise may be blocked as possible spam/phishing attack.	UBE and/or email containing malicious links or attachments may be delivered into user inboxes.	Deployment of domain-based authentication techniques (see Section 4). Use of digital signatures over email (see Section 6).
Email message sent using forged sending address or email address (i.e., phishing, spear phishing).	Loss of reputation, valid email from enterprise may be blocked as possible spam/phishing attack.	UBE and/or email containing malicious links or attachments may be delivered. Users may inadvertently divulge sensitive information or PII.	Deployment of domain-based authentication techniques (see Section 4). Use of digital signatures over email (see Section 6). DNS Blacklists (see Section 7).
Email modified in transit.	Leak of sensitive information or PII.	Leak of sensitive information, altered message may contain malicious information.	Use of TLS to encrypt email transfer between servers (see Section 5). Use of end-to-end email encryption and/or digital signatures (see Section 7). Use of DKIM to identify message mods (see Section 4.5).
Disclosure of sensitive information (e.g., PII) via monitoring and capturing of email traffic.	Leak of sensitive information or PII.	Leak of sensitive information.	Use of TLS to encrypt email transfer between servers (see Section 5). Use of end-to-end email encryption (see Section 7).
Disclosure of metadata of email messages.	Possible privacy violation.	Possible privacy violation.	Use of TLS to encrypt email transfer between servers (see Section 5).

Threat	Impact on Purported Sender	Impact on Receiver	Mitigation
Unsolicited Bulk Email (i.e., spam).	None, unless purported sender is spoofed.	UBE and/or email containing malicious links or attachments may be delivered into user inboxes.	Techniques to address UBE (see Section 7).
DoS/DDoS attack against an enterprises' email servers.	Inability to send email.	Inability to receive email.	Multiple mail servers, use of cloud-based email providers. DNS Blacklists (see Section 7).
Email containing links to malicious site or malware.	None, unless purported sending domain spoofed.	Potential malware installed on enterprise systems.	Techniques to address UBE (Section 7). "Detonation chambers" to open links/attachments for malware scanning, sanitization of attachments, etc. before delivery.

3.5   Security Recommendations Summary

Security Recommendation 3-1: To mitigate the risk of unauthorized sender, an enterprise administrator should block outbound port 25 (except for authorized mail senders) and look to deploy firewall or intrusion detection systems (IDS) that can alert the administrator when an unauthorized host is sending mail via SMTP to the Internet.

Security Recommendation 3-2: Systems that are not involved in the organization's email infrastructure should not be configured to run Mail Transfer Agents (MTAs). Internal systems that need to send mail should be configured to use a trusted internal MSA.

Security Recommendation 3-3: To mitigate the risk of unauthorized receivers, an enterprise administrator should block inbound port 25 and look to deploy firewall or intrusion detection systems (IDS) that can alert the administrator when an unauthorized host is accepting mail via SMTP from the Internet.

4   Authenticating a Sending Domain and Individual Mail Messages

4.1   Introduction

RFC 5322 defines the Internet Message Format (IMF) for delivery over the Simple Mail Transfer Protocol (SMTP) [RFC5321], but in its original state any sender can write any envelope-From: address in the header (see Section 2.3.3). This envelope-From: address can however be overridden by malicious senders or enterprise mail administrators, who may have organizational reasons to rewrite the header, and so both [RFC 5321] and [RFC 5322] defined From: addresses can be aligned to some arbitrary form not intrinsically associated with the originating IP address. In addition, any man in the middle attack can modify a header or data content. New protocols were developed to detect these envelope-From: and message-From: address spoofing or modifications.

Sender Policy Framework (SPF) [RFC4408] uses the Domain Name System (DNS) to allow domain owners to create records that associate the envelope-From: address domain name with one or more IP address blocks used by authorized MTAs. It is then a simple matter for a receiving MTA to check a SPF TXT record in the DNS. This check would confirm the purported sender of a message is in the listed approved sending MTA is indeed authorized to transmit email messages for the domain listed in the envelope-From: address. Mail messages that do not pass this check may be marked, quarantined or rejected. SPF is described in subsection 4.4 below.

The DomainKeys Identified Mail (DKIM) [RFC6376] protocol allows a sending MTA to digitally sign selected headers and the body of the message with a RSA signature and include the signature in a DKIM header that is attached to the message prior to transmission. The DKIM signature header field includes a selector, which the receiver can use to retrieve the public key from a record in the DNS to validate the DKIM signature over the message. So, validating the signature assures the receiver that the message has not been modified in transit – other than additional headers added by MTAs en route which are ignored during the validation. Use of DKIM also ties the email message to the domain publishing the public key, regardless of the From: address (which could be different). DKIM is detailed in subsection 4.5.

Deploying SPF and DKIM may curb illicit activity against a sending domain, but the sender gets no indication of the extent of the beneficial (or otherwise) effects of these policies. Sending domain owners may choose to construct pairwise agreements with selected recipients to manually gather feedback, but this is not a scalable solution. The Domain-based Message Authentication, Reporting and Conformance protocol (DMARC) [RFC7489] institutes such a feedback mechanism, to let sending domain owners know the proportionate effectiveness of their SPF and DKIM policies, and to signal to receivers what action should be taken in various individual and bulk attack scenarios. After setting a policy to advise receivers to deliver, quarantine or reject messages that fail both SPF and DKIM, email receivers then return DMARC aggregate and/or failure reports of email dispositions to the domain owner, who can review the results and potentially refine the policy. DMARC is described in subsection 4.6.

While DMARC can do a lot to curb spoofing and phishing (Section 3.1.6 above), it does need careful configuration. Intermediaries that forward mail have many legitimate reasons to rewrite headers, usually related to legitimate activities such as operating mailing lists, mail groups, and end-user mail forwarding. It should be noted that mail server forwarding changes the source IP address, and without rewriting the envelope-From: address, this can make SPF checks fail. On the other hand, header rewriting, or adding a footer to mail content, may cause the DKIM signature to fail. Both of these interventions can cause problems for DKIM validation and for message delivery. Section 4.6 expands on the problems of mail forwarding, and its mitigations.

SPF, DKIM and DMARC authenticate that the sending MTA is an authorized, legitimate sender of email messages for the domain-part of the envelope-From: (and message-From: for DMARC) address, but these technologies do not verify that the email message is from a specific individual or logical account. That kind of assurance is provided by end-to-end security mechanisms such as S/MIME (or OpenPGP). The DKIM and S/MIME/OpenPGP signature standards are not-interfering: DKIM signatures go in the email header, while S/MIME/OpenPGP signatures are carried as MIME body parts. The signatures are also complementary: a message is typically signed by S/MIME or OpenPGP immediately after it is composed, typically by the sender's MUA, and the DKIM signature is added after the message passes through the sender's MSA or MTA.

The interrelation of SPF, DKIM, DMARC, and S/MIME signatures are shown in the Figure 4-1 below:

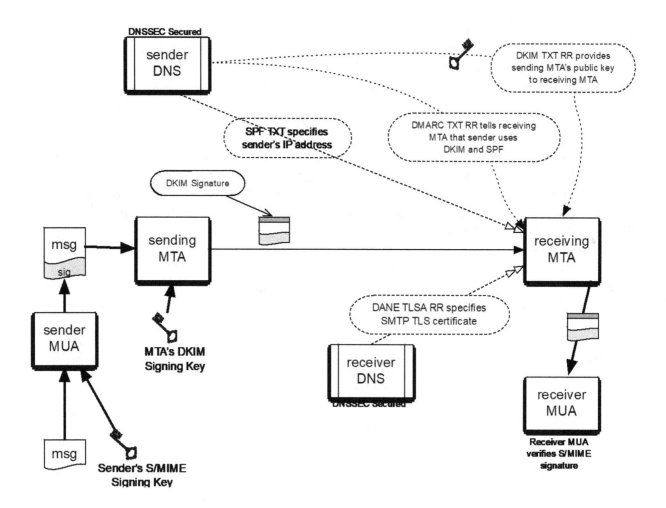

Figure 4-1: The interrelationship of DNSSEC, SPF, DKIM, DMARC and S/MIME for assuring message authenticity and integrity.

4.2 Visibility to End Users

As mentioned above, the domain-based authentication protocols discussed in this section were designed with MTAs in mind. There was thought to be no need for information passed to the end recipient of the email. The results of SPF and DKIM checks are not normally visible in MUA components unless the end user views the message headers directly (and knows how to interpret them). This information may be useful to some end users who wish to filter messages based on these authentication results. [RFC7601] specifics how an MTA/MDA can add a new header to a message upon receipt that provides status information about any authentication checks done by the receiving MTA. Some MUAs make use of this information to provide visual cues (an icon, text color, etc.) to end users that this message passed the MTAs checks and was deemed valid. This does not explicitly mean that the email contents are authentic or valid, just that the email passed the various domain-based checks performed by the receiving MTA.

Email administrators should be aware if the MUAs used in their enterprise can interpret and show results of the authentication headers to end users. Email administrators should educate end users about what the results mean when evaluating potential phishing/spam email as well as not assuming positive results means they have a completely secure channel.

4.3 Requirements for Using Domain-based Authentication Techniques for Federal Systems

As of the time of writing of this guidance document, the DHS has called out the use of domain-based authentication techniques for email as Binding Operational Directive (BOD) 18-01 [BOD18-01]. This includes the techniques discussed below. This section gives best-common-practice guidance of the domain-based authentication techniques listed (but not described) in BOD 18-01 and [FISMAMET]. This document does not extend those requirements in anyway but gives guidance on how to meet existing requirements.

4.4 Sender Policy Framework (SPF)

Sender Policy Framework (SPF) is a standardized way for the domain of the envelope-From: address to identify and assert the mail originators (i.e., mail senders) for a given domain. The sending domain does this by placing a specially formatted Text Resource Record (TXT RR) in the DNS database for the domain. The idea is that a receiving MTA can check the IP address of the connecting MTA against the purported sending domain (the domain-part of the envelope-From: address) and see if the domain vouches for the sending MTA. The receiving MTA does this by sending a DNS query to the purported sending domain for the list of valid senders.

SPF was designed to address phishing and spam being sent by unauthorized senders (i.e., botnets). SPF does not stop all spam, in that spam email being sent from a domain that asserts its sending MTAs via an SPF record will pass all SPF checks. That is, a spammer can send email using an envelope-From: address using a domain that the spammer controls, and that email will not result in a failed SPF check. SPF checks fail when mail is received from a sending MTA other than those listed as approved senders for the envelope-From: domain. For example, an infected botnet of hosts in an enterprise may be sending spam on its own (i.e., not through the enterprises outgoing SMTP server), but those spam messages would be detected as the infected hosts would not be listed as valid senders for the enterprise domain and would fail SPF checks. See [HERZBERG2009] for a detailed review of SPF and its effectiveness.

4.4.1 Background

SPF works by comparing the sender's IP address (IPv4 or IPv6, depending on the transport used to deliver the message) with the policy encoded in any SPF record found at the sending domain. That is, the domain-part of the envelope-From: address. This means that SPF checks can actually be applied before the bulk of the message is received from the sender. For example, in Fig 4-1, the sender with IP address 192.168.0.1 uses the envelope **MAIL FROM**: tag as **alice@example.org** even though the message header is **alice.sender@example.net**. The receiver queries for the SPF RR for example.org and checks if the IP address is listed as a valid sender. If it is listed, or no valid SPF record is found, the message is processed as usual. If not, the receiver may mark the message as a potential spoofed email, quarantine it for further (possibly administrator) analysis or reject the message, depending on the SPF policy and/or the policy discovered in any associated DMARC record (see subsection 4.5, below) for example.org.

```
Client connects to port 25
Server: 220 mx.example.com
Client: HELO mta.example.net
S: 250 Hello mta.example.net, I am glad to meet you
C: MAIL FROM:<alice@example.org>
S: 250 Ok
C: RCPT TO:<bob@example.com>
S: 354 End data with <CR><LF>.<CR><LF>
C: To: bob@example.org
   From: alice.sender@example.net
   Date: Today
   Subject: Meeting today
...
```

Figure 4-2: SMTP envelope header vs. message header

Because of the nature of DNS (which SPF uses for publication) an SPF policy is tied to one domain. That is, **@example.org** and **@sub.example.org** are considered separate domains just like **@example.net** and all three need their own SPF records. This complicates things for organizations that have several domains and subdomains that may (or may not) send mail. There is a way to publish a centralized SPF policy for a collection of domains using the **include**: tag (see Sec 4.2.2.2 below)

SPF was first specified in [RFC4408] as an experimental protocol, since at the same time other, similar proposals were also being considered. Over time however, SPF became widely deployed and was finalized in [RFC7208] (and its updates). The changes between the final version and the original version are mostly minor, and those that base their deployments on the experimental version are still understood by clients that implement the final version. The most significant difference is that the final specification no longer calls for the use of a specialized RRType (simply called a SPF RR) and instead calls for the sender policy to be encoded in a TXT Resource Record, in part because it proved too difficult to universally upgrade legacy DNS systems to accept a new RRType. Older clients may still look for the SPF RR, but the majority will fall back and ask for a TXT RR if it fails to find the special SPF RR. *Resolution of the Sender Policy Framework (SPF) and Sender ID Experiments* [RFC6686] presents the evidence that was used to justify the abandonment of the SPF RR.

SPF is seen as a way to reduce the risk of phishing email being delivered and used as to install malware inside an agency's network. Since it is relatively easy to check using the DNS, SPF is seen as a useful layer of email checks.

4.4.2 SPF on the Sender Side

Deploying SPF for a sending domain is fairly straightforward. It does not even require SPF aware code in mail servers, as receivers, not senders, perform the SPF processing. The only necessary actions are identifying IP addresses or ranges of permitted sending hosts for a given domain and adding that information in the DNS as a new resource record.

4.4.2.1 Identifying Permitted Senders for a Domain and Setting the Policy

The first step in deploying SPF for a sending domain is to identify all the hosts that send email out of the domain (i.e., SMTP servers that are tasked with being email gateways to the Internet). This can be hard to do because:

- There may be mail-sending SMTP servers within sub-units of the organization that are not known to higher-level management.
- There may be other organizations that send mail on behalf of the organization (such as e-mail marketing firms or legitimate bulk-mailers).
- Individuals who work remotely for the organization may send mail using their organization's email address but a local mail relay.

If the senders cannot be listed with certainty, the SPF policy can indicate that receivers should not necessarily reject messages that fail SPF checks by using the "~" or "?" mechanisms, rather than the "-" mechanism (see 4.3.2.2 below) in the SPF TXT record.

Note: Deployment of DMARC [RFC7489] (discussed below) allows for reporting SPF check results back to sending domain owners, which allows senders to modify and improve their policy to minimize improper rejections.

4.4.2.2 Forming the SPF Resource Record

Once all the outgoing senders are identified, the appropriate policy can be encoded and put into the domain database. The SPF syntax is fairly rich and can express complex relationships between senders. Not only can entities be identified and called out, but the SPF statement can also request what emphasis should be placed on each test.

SPF statements are encoded in ASCII text (as they are stored in DNS TXT resource records) and checks are processed in left to right order. Every statement begins with **v=spf1** to indicate that this is an SPF (version 1) statement[8].

Other mechanisms are listed in Table 4-1:

---

[8] Note that there is a technology called SenderID that uses "v=spf2.0", but it is not an updated version of SPF, but a different protocol, not recommended in these guidelines.

Table 4-1: SPF Mechanisms

Tag	Description
ip4:	Specifies an IPv4 address or range of addresses that are authorized senders for a domain.
ip6:	Specifies an IPv6 address or range of addresses that are authorized senders for a domain.
a	Asserts that the IP address listed in the domain's primary A RR is authored to send mail.
mx	Asserts that the listed hosts for the MX RR's are also valid senders for the domain.
include:	Lists another domain where the receiver should look for an SPF RR for further senders. This can be useful for large organizations with many domains or sub-domains that have a single set of shared senders. The **include**: mechanism is recursive, in that the SPF check in the record found is tested in its entirety before proceeding. It is not simply a concatenation of the checks.
all	Matches every IP address that has not otherwise been matched.

Each mechanism in the string is separated by whitespace. In addition, there are qualifiers that can be used for each mechanism (Table 4-2):

Table 4-2: SPF Mechanism Qualifiers

Qualifier	Description
+	The given mechanism check must pass. This is the default mechanism and does not need to be explicitly listed.
-	The given mechanism is not allowed to send email on behalf of the domain.
~	The given mechanism is in transition and if an email is seen from the listed host/IP address, that it should be accepted but marked for closer inspection.
?	The SPF RR explicitly states nothing about the mechanism. In this case, the default behavior is to accept the email. (This makes it equivalent to "+" unless some sort of discrete or aggregate message review is conducted).

There are other mechanisms available as well that are not listed here. Administrators interested in seeing the full depth of the SPF syntax are encouraged to read the full specification in [RFC7208]. To aid administrators, there are some online tools that can be used assist in the generation and testing of an SPF record. These tools take administrator input and generate the text that the administrator then places in a TXT RR in the given domain's zone file.

4.4.2.3　Example SPF RRs

Some examples of the mechanisms for SPF are given below. In each example, the purported sender in the SMTP envelope is **example.com**

The given domain has one mail server that both sends and receives mail. No other system is authorized to send mail. The resulting SPF RR would be:

> **example.com IN TXT "v=spf1 mx -all"**

The given enterprise has a DMZ that allows hosts to send mail but is not sure if other senders exist. As a temporary measure, they list the SPF as:

> **example.com IN TXT "v=spf1 ip4:192.168.1.0/16 ~all"**

The enterprise has several domains for projects, but only one set of sending MTAs. For each domain, there is an SPF RR with the **include:** declaration pointing to a central TXT RR with the SPF policy that covers all the domains. For example, each domain could have:

> **example.com IN TXT "v=spf1 include:spf.example.net."**

The follow up query for the spf.example.net then has:

> **spf.example.net　　　IN TXT "v=spf1 ip4:192.168.0.1 ..."**

This makes SPF easier to manage for an enterprise with several domains and/or public subdomains. Administrators only need to edit **spf.example.net** to make changes to the SPF RR while the other SPF RR's in the other domains simply use the **include:** tag to reference it. No email should originate from the domain:

> **example.com IN TXT "v=spf1 -all"**

The above should be added to all domains that do not send mail to prevent them being used by phishers looking for sending domains to spoof that they believe may not be monitored as closely as those that accept and send enterprise email. This is an important principle for domains that think they are immune from email related threats. Domain names that are only used to host web or services are advised to publish a **"-all"** record, to protect their reputation.

Notice that semicolons are not permitted in the SPF TXT record.

Security Recommendation 4-1: Organizations are recommended to deploy SPF to specify which IP addresses are authorized to transmit email on behalf of the domain. Domains controlled by an organization that are not used to send email, for example Web only domains, should include an SPF RR with the policy indicating that there are no valid email senders for the given domain.

4.4.3   SPF and DNS

Since SPF policies are now only encoded in DNS TXT resource records, no specialized software is needed to host SPF RRs. Organizations can opt to include the old (no longer mandated) unique SPF RRType as well, but it is usually not needed, as clients that still query for the type automatically query for a TXT RR if the SPF RR is not found.

Organizations that deploy SPF should also deploy DNS security (DNSSEC) [RFC4033], [RFC4034], [RFC4035]. DNSSEC provides source authentication and integrity protection for DNS data. SPF RRs in DNSSEC signed zones cannot be altered or stripped from responses without DNSSEC aware receivers detecting the attack. Its use is more fully described in Section 5.

4.4.3.1   Changing an Existing SPF Policy

Changing the policy statement in an SPF RR is straightforward but requires timing considerations due to the caching nature of DNS. It may take some time for the new SPF RR to propagate to all authoritative servers. Likewise, the old, outgoing SPF RR may be cached in client DNS servers for the length of the SPF's TXT RR Time-to-Live (TTL). An enterprise should be aware that some clients might still have the old version of the SPF policy for some time before learning the new version. To minimize the effect of DNS caching, it is useful to decrease the DNS timeout to a small period of time (e.g., 300 seconds) before making changes, and then restoring DNS to a longer time period (e.g., 3600 seconds) after the changes have been made, tested, and confirmed to be correct.

4.4.4   Considerations for SPF when Using Cloud Services or Contracted Services

When an organization outsources its email service (whole or part) to a third party such as a cloud provider or contracted email service, that organization needs to make sure any email sent by those third parties will pass SPF checks. To do this, the enterprise administrator should include the IP addresses of third party senders in the enterprise SPF policy statement RR. Failure to include all the possible senders could result in valid email being rejected due to a failure when doing the SPF check.

Including third-parties to an SPF RR is done by adding the IP addresses/hostnames individually or using the **include:** tag to reference a third party's own SPF record (if one exists). In general, it is preferable to use the **include:** mechanism, as the mechanism avoids hard-coding IP addresses in multiple locations. The **include:** tag does have a hard limit on the number of "chained" **include:** tag that a client will look up to prevent an endless series of queries. This value is ten unique DNS lookups by default.

For instance, if **example.com** has its own sending MTA at 192.0.0.1 but also uses a third party (**third-example.net**) to send non-transactional email as well, the SPF RR for example.com would look like:

example.com IN TXT   "v=spf1 ip4:192.0.0.1
include:third-example.net -all"

As mentioned above, the **include:** mechanism does not simply concatenate the policy tests of the included domain (here: **third-example.net**) but performs all the checks in the SPF policy referenced and returns the final result. An administrator should not include the modifier "**+**" (requiring the mechanism to pass in order for the whole check to pass) to the **include:** unless they are also in control of the included domain, as any change to the SPF policy in the included domain will affect the SPF validation check for the sending domain.

4.4.5   SPF on the Receiver Side

Unlike senders, receivers need to have SPF-aware mail servers to check SPF policies. SPF has been around in some form (either experimental or finalized) and available in just about all major mail server implementations. There are also patches and libraries available for other implementations to make them SPF-aware and perform SPF queries and processing[9]. There may be plug-ins available for a particular Mail User Agent so end users can perform SPF checks even if their incoming mail server does not.

As mentioned above, SPF uses the envelope-From: address domain-part and the IP address of the sender. This means that SPF checks can be started before the actual text of the email message is received. Alternatively, messages can be quickly received and held in quarantine until all the checks are finished. In either event, checks must be completed before the mail message is sent to an end user's inbox (unless the only SPF checks are performed by the end user using their own MUA).

The resulting action based on the SPF checks depends on local receiver policy and the statements in the purported sending domain's SPF statement. The action should be based on the modifiers (listed above) on each mechanism. If no SPF TXT RR is returned in the query, or the SPF has formatting errors that prevent parsing, the default behavior is to accept the message. This is the same behavior for mail servers that are not SPF-aware.

4.4.5.1   SPF Queries and DNS

Just as an organization that deploys SPF should also deploy DNSSEC [SP800-81], receivers that perform SPF processing should also perform DNSSEC validation (if possible) on responses to SPF queries. A mail server should be able to send queries to a validating DNS recursive server if it cannot perform its own DNSSEC validation.

---

[9] A list of some SPF implementations can be found at http://www.openspf.org/Implementations.

Security Recommendation 4-2: Organizations should deploy DNSSEC for all DNS name servers and validate DNSSEC responses on all systems that receive email.

4.5   DomainKeys Identified Mail (DKIM)

DomainKeys Identified Mail (DKIM) permits a person, role, or organization that owns the signing domain to claim some responsibility for a message by associating the domain with the message. This can be an author's organization, an operational relay, or one of their agents. DKIM separates the question of the identity of the signer of the message from the purported author of the message. Assertion of responsibility is validated through a cryptographic signature and by querying the signer's domain directly to retrieve the appropriate public key. Message transit from author to recipient is through relays that typically make no substantive change to the message content and thus preserve the DKIM signature. Because the DKIM signature covers the message body, it also protects the integrity of the email communication. Changes to a message body will result in a DKIM signature validation failure, which is why some mailing lists (that add footers to email messages or change Subject header fields) will cause DKIM signature validation failures (discussed below).

A DKIM signature is generated by the signing MTA using the email message body and headers and places it in the header of the message along with information for the client to use in validation of the signature (i.e., key selector, algorithm, etc.). When the receiving MTA gets the message, it attempts to validate the signature by looking for the public key indicated in the DKIM signature. The MTA issues a DNS query for a text resource record (TXT RR) that contains the encoded key.

Like SPF (see Section 4.4), DKIM allows an enterprise to vouch for an email message sent from a domain it does not control (as would be listed in the SMTP envelope). The sender only needs the private key to generate signatures. This allows an enterprise to have email sent on its behalf by an approved third party. The presence of the public key in the enterprises' DNS implies that there is a relationship between the enterprise and the sender.

Since DKIM requires the use cryptographic keys, enterprises must have a key management plan in place to generate, store and retire key pairs. Administrative boundaries complicate this plan if one organization sends mail on another organization's behalf.

4.5.1   Background

DKIM was originally developed as part of a private sector consortium and only later transitioned to an IETF standard. The threat model that the DKIM protocol is designed to protect against was published as [RFC4686] and assumes bad actors with an extensive corpus of mail messages from the domains being impersonated, knowledge of the businesses being impersonated, access to business public keys, and the ability to submit messages to MTAs and MSAs at many locations across the Internet. The original DKIM protocol specification was developed as [RFC4871], which is now considered obsolete. The specification underwent several revisions and updates and the current version of the DKIM specification is published as [RFC6376].

4.5.2   DKIM on the Sender Side

Unlike SPF, DKIM requires specialized functionality on the sender MTA to generate the signatures. Therefore, the first step in deploying DKIM is to ensure that the organization has an MTA that can support the generation of DKIM signatures. DKIM support is currently available in some implementations or can be added using open source filters[10]. Administrators should remember that since DKIM involves digital signatures, signing MTAs should also have appropriate cryptographic tools to create and store keys and perform cryptographic operations.

4.5.3   Generation and Distribution of the DKIM Key Pair

The next step in deploying DKIM, after ensuring that the sending MTA is DKIM-aware, is to generate a signing key pair.

Cryptographic keys should be generated in accordance with NIST SP 800-57, "Recommendations for Key Management" [SP800-57pt1] and NIST SP 800-133, "Recommendations for Cryptographic Key Generation." [SP800-133] Although there exist web-based systems for generating DKIM public/private key pairs and automatically producing the corresponding DNS entries, such systems should not be used for federal information systems because they may compromise the organization's private key.

Currently the DKIM standard specifies that messages must be signed with one of two digital signature algorithms: RSA/SHA-256 and the Edwards-curve Digital Signature Algorithm Curve25519 (ed25519) [RFC8463]. Of these, only RSA/SHA-256 is approved for use by government agencies with DKIM, as the hash algorithm SHA-1 is no longer approved for use in conjunction with digital signatures (see Table 4-3).

Table 4-3: Recommended Cryptographic Key Parameters

DKIM Specified Algorithm	Approved for Government Use?	Recommended Length	Recommended Lifetime
RSA/SHA-256	YES	2048 bits	1-2 years
ed25519	NO[11]	256 bits	N/A

Once the key pair is generated, the administrator should determine a selector name to use with the key. A DKIM selector name is a unique identifier for the key that is used to distinguish one DKIM key from any other potential keys used by the same sending domain, allowing different MTAs to be configured with different signing keys. This selector name is used by receiving MTAs to query the validating key.

---

[10] Mail filters are sometimes called "milters." A milter is a process subordinate to a MTA that can be deployed to perform special message header or body processing.

[11] As of the time of writing, ed25519 is being considered for approval, but has not been approved for use for federal systems.

The public part of the key pair is stored in a the DKIM TXT Resource Record (RR). This record should be added to the organization's DNS server and tested to make sure that it is accessible both within and outside the organization.

The private part of the key pair is used by the MTA to sign outgoing mail. Administrators must configure their mail systems to protect the private part of the key pair from exposure to prevent an attacker from learning the key and using it to spoof email with the victim domain's DKIM key. For example, if the private part of the key pair is kept in a file, file permissions must be set so that only the user under which the MTA is running can read it.

As with any cryptographic keying material, enterprises should use a Cryptographic Key Management System (CKMS) to manage the generation, distribution, and lifecycle of DKIM keys. Federal agencies are encouraged to consult NIST SP 800-130 [SP800-130] and NIST SP 800-152 [SP800-152] for guidance on how to design and implement a CKMS within an agency.

Security Recommendation 4-3: Federal agency administrators shall only use keys with approved algorithms and lengths for use with DKIM.

Security Recommendation 4-4: Administrators should ensure that the private portion of the key pair is adequately protected on the sending MTA and that only the MTA software has read privileges for the key. Federal agency administrators should follow FISMA control SC-12 [SP800-53] guidance with regards to distributing and protecting DKIM key pairs.

Security Recommendation 4-5: Each sending MTA should be configured with its own private key and its own selector value, to minimize the damage that may occur if a private key is compromised. This private key must have protection against both accidental disclosure or attacker's attempt to obtain or modify.

4.5.4 Example of a DKIM Signature

Below is an example of a DKIM signature as would be seen in an email header. A signature is made up of a collection of **tag=value** pairs that contain parameters needed to successfully validate the signature as well as the signature itself. An administrator usually cannot configure the tags individually as these are done by the MTA functionality that does DKIM, though some require configuration (such as the selector, discussed above). Some common tags are described in Table 4-4.

Table 4-4: DKIM Signature Tag and Value Descriptions

Tag	Name	Description
v=	Version	Version of DKIM in use by the signer. Currently the only defined value is "**1**".
a=	Algorithm	The algorithm used (**rsa-sha1** or **rsa-sha256**)
b=	Signature ("base")	The actual signature encoded as a base64 string in textual representations

Tag	Name	Description
bh=	Signature Hash ("base hash")	The hash of the body of the email message encoded as a base64 string.
d=	Domain	The DNS name of the party vouching for the signature. This is used to identify the DNS domain where the public key resides.
i=	Identifier	The identifier is normally either the same as, or a subdomain of, the d= domain.
s=	Selector	Required selector value. This, together with the domain identified in the **d=** tag, is used to form the DNS query used to obtain the key that can validate the DKIM signature.
t=	Timestamp	The time the DKIM signature was generated.
x=	Signature expiration	An optional value to state a time after which the DKIM signature should no longer be considered valid. Often included to provide anti-replay protection.
l=	Length	Length specification for the body in octets. So the signature can be computed over a given length, and this will not affect authentication in the case that a mail forwarder adds an additional suffix to the message.

Thus, a DKIM signature from a service provider sending mail on behalf of **example.gov** might appear as an email header:

> **DKIM-Signature: v=1; a=rsa-sha256; d=example.gov; c=simple; i=@gov-sender.example.gov; t=1425066098; s=adkimkey; bh=***base64 string***; b=***base64 string***

Note that DKIM requires the use of semicolons between statements.

4.5.5   Generation and Provisioning of the DKIM Resource Record

The public portion of the DKIM key is encoded into a DNS TXT Resource Record (RR) and published in the zone indicated in the FROM: field of the email header. The DNS name for the RR uses the selector the administrator chose for the key pair and a special tag to indicate it is for DKIM ("**_domainkey**"). For example, if the selector value for the DKIM key used with example.gov is "dkimkey", then the resulting DNS RR has the name **dkimkey._domainkey.example.gov**.

Like SPF, there are other **tag=value** pairs that need to be included in a DKIM RR. The full list of tags is listed in the specification [RFC6376], but relevant ones are listed below:

Table 4-5: DKIM RR Tag and Value Descriptions

Tag	Name	Description
v=	Version	Version of DKIM in use with the domain and required for every DKIM RR. The default value is "**DKIM1**".
k=	Key type	The default is **rsa** and is optional, as RSA is currently the only specified algorithm used with DKIM
p=	Public Key	The encoded public key (base64 encoded in text zone files). An empty value indicates that the key with the given selector field has been revoked.
t=	Optional flags	One defined flag is "**y**" indicating that the given domain is experimenting with DKIM and signals to clients to treat signed messages as unsigned (to prevent messages that failed validation from being dropped). The other is "**s**" to signal that there must be a direct match between the "**d=**" tag and the "**i=**" tag in the DKIM signature. That is, the "**i=**" tag must not be a subdomain of the "**d=**" tag.

4.5.6 Example of a DKIM RR

Below is an example for the DKIM key that would be used to validate the DKIM signature above. Here, not all the flags are given:

adkimkey._domainkey.example.gov. IN TXT "v=DKIM1; k=rsa;
                                            p=<*base64 string*>"

Note that unlike SPF, DKIM requires the use of semicolons between statements in a DNS RR.

4.5.7 DKIM and DNS

Since DKIM public keys are encoded in DNS TXT resource records, no specialized software is needed to host DKIM public keys. Organizations that deploy DKIM should also deploy DNS security (DNSSEC) [RFC4033] [RFC4034] [RFC4035]. DNSSEC provides source authentication and integrity protection for DNS data. This prevents attackers from spoofing or intercepting and deleting responses for receivers' DKIM key TXT queries.

Security Recommendation 4-6: Organizations should deploy DNSSEC to provide authentication and integrity protection to the DKIM DNS resource records.

4.5.8 DKIM Operational Considerations

There are several operations an email administrator will need to perform to maintain DKIM for an email service. New email services are acquired; DKIM keys are introduced, rolled (i.e., changed), and eventually retired, etc. Since DKIM requires the use of DNS, administrators need to take the nature of DNS into account when performing maintenance operations. [RFC5863] describes the complete set of maintenance operations for DKIM in detail, but the three most common operations are summarized below.

4.5.8.1 Introduction of a New DKIM Key

When initially deploying DKIM for enterprise email, or a new email service to support an organization, an administrator should insure that the corresponding public key is available for validation. Thus, the DNS entry with the DKIM public portion should be published in the sender's domain before the sending MTA begins using the private portion to generate signatures. The order should be:

1. Generate a DKIM key pair and determine the selector that will be used by the MTA(s).
2. Generate and publish the DKIM TXT RR in the sending domain's DNS.
3. Ensure that the DKIM TXT RR is returned in queries.
4. Configure the sending MTA(s) to use the private portion.
5. Begin using the DKIM key pair with email.

4.5.8.2 Changing an Active DKIM Key Pair

DKIM keys may change for various purposes: suspected weakness or compromise, scheduled policy, change in operator, or because the DKIM key has reached the end of its lifetime.

Changing, or rolling, a DKIM key pair consists of introducing a new DKIM key before its use and keeping the old, outgoing key in the DNS long enough for clients to obtain it to validate signatures. This requires multiple DNS changes with a wait time between them. The relevant steps are:

1. Generate a new DKIM key pair.
2. Generate a new DKIM TXT RR, with a different selector value than the outgoing DKIM key and publish it in the enterprise's DNS. *At this point, the DNS will be serving both the old and the new DKIM entries.*
3. Reconfigure the sending MTA(s) to use the new DKIM key.
4. Validate the correctness of the public key.
5. Begin using the new DKIM key for signature generation.
6. Wait a period of time.
7. Delete the outgoing DKIM TXT RR.
8. Delete or archive the retired DKIM key according to enterprise policy.

The necessary period of time to wait before deleting the outgoing DKIM key's TXT RR cannot be a universal constant value due to the nature of DNS and SMTP (i.e., mail queuing). An enterprise cannot be certain when all of its email has passed DKIM checks using its old key. An old DKIM key could still be queried for by a receiving MTA for hours (or potentially days) after the email had been sent. Therefore, the outgoing DKIM key should be kept in the DNS for a period of time (potentially a week) before final deletion.

If it is necessary to revoke or delete a DKIM key, it can be immediately retired by either be removing the key's corresponding DKIM TXT RR or by altering the RR to have a blank **p=**. Either achieves the same effect (the client can no longer validate the signature) but keeping the DKIM RR with a blank **p=** value explicitly signals that the key has been removed.

Revoking a key is similar to deleting it but the enterprise may pre-emptively delete (or change) the DKIM RR before the sender has stopped using it. This scenario is possible when an enterprise wishes to break DKIM authentication and does not control the sender (i.e., a third party or rogue sender). In these scenarios, the enterprise can delete or change the DKIM RR in order to break validation of DKIM signatures. Additional deployment of DMARC (see Section 4.5) can be used to indicate that this DKIM validation failure should result in the email being rejected or deleted.

4.5.9   DKIM on the Receiver Side

On the receiver side, email administrators should first make sure their MTA implementation has the functionality to verify DKIM signatures. Most major implementations have the functionality built-in or can be included using open source patches or a mail filter (i.e., milter). In some cases, the administrator may need to install additional cryptographic libraries to perform the actual validation.

4.5.9.1   DKIM Queries in the DNS

Just as an organization that deploys DKIM should deploy DNSSEC, receivers that perform DKIM processing should also perform DNSSEC validation (if possible) on responses to DKIM TXT queries. A mail server should be able to send queries to a validating DNS recursive server if it cannot perform its own DNSSEC validation.

Security Recommendation 4-7: Organizations should enable DNSSEC validation on DNS servers used by MTAs that verify DKIM signatures.

4.5.10 Issues with Mailing Lists

DKIM assumes that the email came from the MTA domain that generated the signature. This presents some problems when dealing with certain mailing lists. Often, MTAs that process mailing lists change the bodies of mailing list messages—for example, adding a footer with mailing list information or similar. Such actions are likely to invalidate DKIM signatures, unless for example, a message length is specified in the signature headers, and the additions come beyond that length.

Fundamentally, mailing lists act as active mail parties. They receive messages from senders and resend them to recipients. Sometimes they send messages as they are received, sometimes the messages are bundled and sent as a single combined message, and sometimes recipients are able to choose their delivery means. As such, mailing lists should verify the DKIM signatures of incoming messages, and then re-sign outgoing messages with their own DKIM signature, made with the MTA's public/private key pair. See [RFC6377], "DomainKeys Identified Mail (DKIM) and Mailing Lists," also identified as IETF BCP 167, for additional discussion of DKIM and mailing lists.

Additional assurance can be obtained by providing mailing lists with a role-based (i.e., not a named individual) S/MIME certificate and digitally signing outgoing. Such signatures will allow verification of the mailing list signature using S/MIME aware clients such as Microsoft Outlook, Mozilla Thunderbird, and Apple Mail. See Sections 2.4.2 and 4.7 for a discussion of S/MIME. Signatures are especially important for broadcast mailing lists that are sent with message-From: addresses that are not monitored, such as "do-not-reply" email addresses.

Security Recommendation 4-8: Mailing list software should verify DKIM signatures on incoming mail and re-sign outgoing mail with new DKIM signatures.

Security Recommendation 4-9: Mail sent to broadcast mailing lists from do-not-reply or unmonitored mailboxes should be digitally signed with S/MIME signatures so that recipients can verify the authenticity of the messages.

As with SPF (subsection 4.2 above), DKIM does not prevent a spammer/advertiser from using a legitimately obtained domain to send unsolicited, DKIM-signed email. DKIM is used to provide assurance that the purported sender is the originator of the message, and that the message has not been modified in transit by an unauthorized intermediary.

4.5.11 Considerations for Enterprises When Using Cloud or Contracted Email Services

An enterprise that uses third party senders for email services needs to have a policy in place for DKIM key management. The nature of DKIM requires that the sending MTA have the private key in order to generate signatures while the domain owner may only have the public portion. This makes key management controls difficult to audit and or impossible to enforce. Compartmentalizing DKIM keys is one approach to minimize risk when sharing keying material between organizations.

When using DKIM with cloud or contracted services, an enterprise should generate a unique key pair for each service. No private key should be shared between contracted services or cloud instances. This includes the enterprise itself, if email is sent by MTAs operated within the enterprise.

Security Recommendation 4-10: A unique DKIM key pair should be used for each third party that sends email on the organization's behalf.

Likewise, at the end of contract lifecycle, all DKIM keys published by the enterprise must be deleted or modified to have a blank **p=** field to indicate that the DKIM key has been revoked. This prevents the third party from continuing to send DKIM validated email.

4.6 Domain-based Message Authentication, Reporting and Conformance (DMARC)

SPF and DKIM were created so that email sending domain owners could give guidance to receivers about whether mail purporting to originate from them was valid, and thus whether it should be delivered, flagged, or discarded. Both SPF and DKIM offer implementation flexibility and different settings can have different effects at the receiver. However, neither SPF nor DKIM include a mechanism to tell receivers if SPF or DKIM are in active use, nor do they have feedback mechanism to inform sending domain owners of the effectiveness of their authentication techniques. For example, if a message arrives at a receiver without a DKIM signature, DKIM provides no mechanism to allow the receiver to learn if the message is authentic but was sent from a sender that did not implement DKIM, or if the message is a spoof.

DMARC [RFC7489] allows email sending domain owners to specify policy on how receivers can verify the authenticity of their email, how the receiver can handle email that fails to verify, and the frequency and types of report that receivers should send back. DMARC benefits receivers by removing the guesswork about which security protocols are in use, allowing more certainty in quarantining and rejecting inauthentic mail.

To further improve authentication, DMARC adds a link between the domain of the sender with the authentication results for SPF and DKIM. In particular, receivers compare the domain in the message-From: address in the message to the SPF and DKIM results (if deployed) and the DMARC policy in the DNS. The results of this data gathering are used to determine how the mail should be handled. Thus, when an email fails SPF and DKIM verification, or the message-From: domain-part doesn't match the authentication results, the email can be treated as inauthentic according to the sending domain owners DMARC policy.

DMARC also provides a mechanism that allows receivers to send reports to the domain owner about mail claiming to originate from their domain. These reports can be used to illuminate the extent to which unauthorized users are using the domain, and the proportion of mail received that is from the purported sender.

4.6.1   DMARC on the Sender Side

DMARC policies work in conjunction with SPF and/or DKIM, so a mail domain owner intending to deploy DMARC must deploy SPF or DKIM or (preferably) both. To deploy DMARC, the sending domain owner will publish SPF and/or DKIM RRs in the DNS and calculate a signature for the DKIM header of every outgoing message. The domain owner also publishes a DMARC policy in the DNS advising receivers on how to treat messages purporting to originate from the sender's domain. The domain owner does this by publishing its DMARC policy as a TXT record in the DNS[12]; identified by creating a **_dmarc** DNS record and publishing it in the sending domain name. For example, the DMARC policy for "example.gov" would reside at the fully qualified domain name **_dmarc.example.gov**.

When implementing email authentication for a domain for the first time, a sending domain owner is advised to first publish a DMARC RR with a "none" policy before deploying SPF or DKIM. This allows the sending domain owner to immediately receive reports indicating the volume of

---

[12] Example tool: https://dmarcguide.globalcyberalliance.org/

email being sent that purports to be from their domain. These reports can be used in crafting an email authentication policy that reduces the risk of errors.

Since the sending domain owner will be soliciting feedback reports by email from receivers, the administrator should establish email addresses to receive aggregate and failure reports. As the DMARC RR is easily discovered, the reporting inboxes could be subject to voluminous unsolicited bulk email (i.e., spam). Therefore, some kind of abuse counter-measures for these email in-boxes should be deployed.

Even if a sending domain owner does not deploy SPF or DKIM records it may be useful to deploy a DMARC record with policy **p=none** and a **rua** tag, to encourage receivers to send aggregate reports about the use to which the sender's domain is being put. This can help with preliminary evaluation to determine whether a mail sender should mount SPF and DKIM defenses.

4.6.2 The DMARC DNS Record

The DMARC policy is encoded in a TXT record placed in the DNS by the sending domain owner. Similar to SPF and DKIM, the DMARC policy is encoded in a series of **tag=value** pairs separated by semicolons. Common keys are:

Table 4-6: DMARC RR Tag and Value Descriptions

Tag	Name	Description
v=	Version	Version field that must be present as the first element. By default, the value is always **DMARC1**.
p=	Policy	Mandatory policy field. May take values **none** or **quarantine** or **reject**. This allows for a gradually tightening policy where the sender domain recommends no specific action on mail that fails DMARC checks (**p=none**), through treating failed mail as suspicious (**p=quarantine**), to rejecting all failed mail (**p=reject**), preferably at the SMTP transaction stage.
aspf=	SPF Policy	Values are "**r**" (default) for relaxed and "**s**" for strict SPF domain enforcement. Strict alignment requires an exact match between the message-From: address domain and the (passing) SPF check must exactly match the RFC envelope-From: address (i.e., the HELO address). Relaxed requires that only the message-From: and envelope-From: address domains be in alignment. For example, the envelope-From: address domain-part "**smtp.example.org**" and the message-From: address "**announce@example.org**" are in alignment, but not a strict match.

Tag	Name	Description
adkim=	DKIM Policy	Optional. Values are "**r**" (default) for relaxed and "**s**" for strict DKIM domain enforcement. Strict alignment requires an exact match between the message-From: domain in the message header and the DKIM domain presented in the "**d=**" DKIM tag. Relaxed requires only that the domain part is in alignment (as in **aspf** above).
fo=	Failure Reporting options	Optional. Ignore if a "**ruf**" argument below is not also present. Value **0** indicates the receiver should generate a DMARC failure report if all underlying mechanisms fail to produce an aligned "pass" result. Value **1** means generate a DMARC failure report if any underlying mechanism produces something other than an aligned "pass" result. Other possible values are "**d**" and "**s**": "**d**" means generate a DKIM failure report if a signature failed evaluation. "**s**" means generate an SPF failure report if the message failed SPF evaluation. These values are not exclusive and may be combined together in a colon-separated list.
ruf=		Optional. Lists a series of Universal Resource Indicators (URI's) (currently just "**mailto:<emailaddress>**") that list where to send failure feedback reports. This is for reports on message specific failures. Sending domain owners should use this argument sparingly, since it is used to request a report on a per-failure basis, which could result in a large volume of failure reports.
rua=		Optional list of URI's (like in **ruf=** above, using the "**mailto:**" URI) listing where to send aggregate feedback back to the sending domain owner. These reports are sent based on the interval requested using the "**ri=**" option below, with a default of 86400 seconds if not listed.
ri=	Reporting Interval	Optional with the default value of 86400 seconds (one day). The value listed is the reporting interval desired by the sending domain owner.

Tag	Name	Description
pct=	Percent	Optional with the default value of **100**(%). Expresses the percentage of a sending domain owner's mail that should be subject to the given DMARC policy in a range from 0 to 100. This allows domain owners to ramp up their policy enforcement gradually and prevent having to commit to a rigorous policy before getting feedback on their existing policy. Note: this value must be an integer.
sp=	Subdomain Policy	Optional with a default value of **none**. Other values include the same range of values as the '**p=**' argument. This is the policy to be applied to mail from all identified subdomains of the given DMARC RR. If a receiver fails to find a valid DMARC RR for a given sending domain, it will attempt to find a DMARC RR for a parent zone and apply a DMARC policy if the **sp=** tag is present.

Like SPF and DKIM, the DMARC record is actually a DNS TXT RR. Like all DNS information, it should be signed using DNSSEC [RFC4033], [RFC4034], and [RFC4035] to prevent an attacker from spoofing the DNS response and altering the DMARC check by a client.

4.6.3 Example of DMARC RR's

Below are several examples of DMARC policy records using the above tags. The most basic example is a DMARC policy that effectively does not assert anything and does not request the receiver send any feedback reports, so it is, in effect, useless.

    _dmarc.example.gov 3600 IN TXT "v=DMARC1; p=none;"

An agency that is preparing to deploy SPF and/or DKIM, or has deployed these technologies, but may not be confident in their current policies may request aggregate reports from receivers, but otherwise advises no specific action. The agency can do so by publishing a **p=none** policy as in the example below.

    _dmarc.example.gov 3600 IN TXT "v=DMARC1; p=none;
                        rua=reports@example.gov;"

An agency that has deployed SPF and DKIM and advises receivers to reject any messages that fail these checks would publish a **p=reject** policy as in the example below. Here, the agency also wishes to receive aggregate reports on a daily basis (the default).

    _dmarc.example.gov 3600 IN TXT "v=DMARC1; p=reject;
                        rua=reports@example.gov;"

The agency in the process of deploying DKIM (but has confidence in their SPF policy) may wish to receive feedback solely on DKIM failures, but does not wish to be inundated with feedback, so requests that the policy be applied to a subset of messages received. In this case, the DMARC policy would include the **fo=** option to indicate only DKIM failures are to be reported and a **pct=** value of **10** to indicate that only 1 in 10 email messages should be subjected to this policy (and subsequent reporting on a failure). Note that this is not a wise strategy in that it reduces the enforcement policy and the completeness of reporting. The use of the **pct** value in values other than 0 or 100 (i.e., none or full) limits DMARC effectiveness and usefulness of reporting. It is also burdensome for receivers to choose that intermediate percentage of mail for testing.

_dmarc.example.gov 3600 IN TXT "v=DMARC1; p=none; pct=10; fo=d; ruf=reports@example.gov;"

An agency with several subdomains may wish to have a single unified policy, in which case a DMARC RR with the **sp=** tag is used. In this example, the domain has a policy to reject any mail from a subdomain of example.gov that fails checks, while only quarantining email that failed checks from the parent domain.

_dmarc.example.gov   3600 IN TXT "v=DMARC1; p=quarantine; sp=reject; rua=reports@example.gov;"

Security Recommendation 4-11: Sending domain owners who deploy SPF and/or DKIM are recommended to publish a DMARC record signaling to mail receivers the disposition expected for messages purporting to originate from the sender's domain.

4.6.4   DMARC on the Receiver Side

Receivers of email purporting to originate from a given domain will look up the SPF, DKIM and DMARC records in the DNS and act on the policies encoded therein. The recommended processing order per [RFC7489] is given below. Note that it is possible that some steps could be done in parallel and local policy may alter the order of some steps (i.e., steps 2, 3 and 4).

1. The receiver extracts the message-From: address from the message. This must contain a single, valid address or else the mail is refused as an error.
2. The receiver queries for the DMARC DNS record based on the message-From: address. If none exists, terminate DMARC processing. This may include queries to any potential parent zone of the sender.
3. The receiver performs DKIM signature checks. If more than one DKIM signature exists in the message, one must verify.
4. The receiver queries for the sending domain's SPF record and performs SPF validation checks.
5. The receiver conducts Identifier Alignment checks between the message-From: and the results of the SPF and DKIM records (if present). It does so by comparing the domain extracted from the message-From: (as in step 2 above) with the domain in the verified

SPF and/or DKIM verification steps. If there is a match with either the domain verified by SPF or DKIM, then the DMARC Identifier Alignment check passes.

6. The receiver applies the DMARC policy found in the purported sender's DMARC record unless it conflicts with the receiver's local policy. The receiver will also store the results of evaluating each received message for the purpose of compiling aggregate reports sent back to the domain owner (as specified in the **rua** tag).

Note that local email processing policy may override a sending domain owner's stated DMARC policy. The receiver should also store the results of evaluating each received message in some persistent form for the purpose of compiling aggregate reports.

Even if steps 2-5 in the above procedure yield no SPF or DKIM records to evaluate the message, it is still useful to send aggregate reports based on the sending domain owner's DMARC preferences, as it helps shape sending domain responses to spam in the system.

Security Recommendation 4-12: Mail receivers who evaluate SPF and DKIM results of received messages are recommended to dispose them in accordance with the sending domain's published DMARC policy, if any. They are also recommended to initiate failure reports and aggregate reports according to the sending domain's DMARC policies.

4.6.5 Policy and Reporting

DMARC can be seen as consisting of two components: a policy on linking SPF and DKIM checks to the message-From: address, and a reporting mechanism. The reason for DMARC reporting is so that domain owners can get feedback on their SPF, DKIM, Identifier Alignment and message disposition policies so these can be made more effective. The DMARC protocol specifies a system of aggregate reports sent by receivers on a periodic basis, and failure reports sent on a message-by-message basis for email that fail some component part of the DMARC checks. The specified form in which receivers send aggregate reports is as a compressed (zipped) XML file based on the AFRF format [RFC6591], [RFC7489][13]. Each aggregate report from a mail receiver back to a particular domain owner includes aggregate figures for successful and unsuccessful message authentications including:

- The sending domain owner's DMARC policy for that interval (domain owners may change policies and it is undetermined whether a receiver will respond based on the old policy or the new policy).
- The message disposition by the receiver (i.e., delivered, quarantined, rejected).
- SPF result for a given SPF identifier.
- DKIM result for a given DKIM identifier.
- Whether identifiers are in alignment or not.

---

[13] Appendix C of RFC 7489.

- Results classified by sender subdomain (whether or not a separate **sp** policy exists).
- The sending and receiving domain pair.
- The policy applied, and whether this is different from the policy requested.
- The number of successful authentications.
- Totals for all messages received.

Based on the return flow of aggregate reports from the aggregation of all receivers, a domain owner can build up a picture of the email being sent and how it appears to outside receivers. This allows the domain owner to identify gaps in email infrastructure and policy and how (and when) it can be improved. In the early stages of building up this picture, the sending domain should set a DMARC policy of **p=none**, so the ultimate disposition of a message that fails some checks rests wholly on the receiver's local policy. As DMARC aggregate reports are collected, the domain owner will have a quantitatively better assessment of the extent to which the sender's email is authenticated by outside receivers and will be able to set a policy of **p=reject**, indicating that any message that fails the SPF, DKIM and alignment checks really should be rejected via a SMTP reply code signaling rejection, or silently discarding the message. Note, however, mailing lists and some other email uses (e.g., "share this post" type links) may fail DMARC validation and may need to be considered when forming a policy. From their own traffic analysis, receivers can develop a determination of whether a sending domain owner's **p=reject** policy is sufficiently trustworthy to act on.

Failure reports from receivers to domain owners help debug and tune the component SPF and DKIM mechanisms as well as alerting the domain owner that their domain is being used as part of a phishing/spam campaign. Typical initial rollout of DMARC in an enterprise will include the **ruf** tag with the values of the **fo** tag progressively modified to capture SPF debugging, DKIM debugging or alignment debugging. Failure reports are expensive to produce and bear a real danger of providing a DDoS source back to domain owners, so when sufficient confidence is gained in the integrity of the component mechanisms, the **ruf** tag may be dropped from DMARC policy statements if the sending domain no longer wants to receive failure reports. Note however that failure reports can also be used to alert domain owners about phishing attacks being launched using their domain as the purported sender and therefore dropping the **ruf** tag is not recommended.

The same AFRF report format as for aggregate reports [RFC6591], [RFC7489] is also specified for failure reports, but the DMARC standard updates it for the specificity of a single failure report:

- Receivers include as much of the message and message header as is reasonable to allow the domain to investigate the failure.
- Add an Identity-Alignment field, with DKIM and SPF DMARC-method fields as appropriate (see above).
- Optionally add a Delivery-Result field.
- Add DKIM Domain, DKIM Identity and DKIM selector fields, if the message was DKIM signed. Optionally also add DKIM Canonical header and body fields.

- Add an additional DMARC authentication failure type, for use when some authentication mechanisms fail to produce aligned identifiers.

4.6.6 Considerations for Agencies When Using Cloud or Contracted Email Services

The **rua** and **ruf** tags typically specify **mailto:** addresses in the sender's domain. These reporting addresses are normally assumed to be in the same domain as the purported sender, but not always. Cloud providers and contracted services may provide DMARC report collection as part of their service offerings. In these instances, the **mailto:** domain will differ from the sending domain. To prevent DMARC reporting being used as a DoS vector, the owner of the **mailto:** domain must signal its legitimacy by posting a DMARC TXT DNS record with the Fully Qualified Domain Name (FQDN):

*original-sender-domain.***_report._dmarc.***mailto-domain*

For example, an original message sent from **example.gov** is authenticated with a DMARC record:

**_dmarc.example.gov. IN TXT "v=DMARC1; p=reject;
rua=mailto:reports.example.net"**

The recipient then queries for a DMARC TXT RR at
example.gov._report._dmarc.example.net and checks the **rua** tag includes the value
rua=mailto:reports.example.net to ensure that the address specified in the sending domain
owner's DMARC record is the legitimate receiver for DMARC reports.

Note that, as with DKIM, DMARC records require the use of semicolons between tags.

4.6.7 Mail Forwarding and Indirect Email Flows

The message authentication devices of SPF, DKIM and DMARC are designed to work directly between a sender domain and a receiver domain. The message envelope and RFC5322.From address pass through a series of MTAs and are authenticated by the receiver. The DKIM signature, message headers and message body arrive at the receiver unchanged. The email system has additional complexities as there are a variety of message forwarding activity that will very often either modify the message or change the apparent message-From: domain. For example, **user@example.gov** sends a message to **ourgroup@example.net**, which is subsequently forwarded to all members of the mail group. If the mail group software simply relays the message, the envelope-From: address denoting the forwarder differs from the message-From: address, denoting the original sender. In this case DMARC processing will rely on DKIM for authentication. If the forwarder modifies the message-From: field to match the HELO of the sending MTA (see Section 2.3.1), SPF may authenticate, but the modified header will make the DKIM signature invalid.

Another example is the use of some third-party email scanning services. In cases where email is received by a domain, and then "shunted" to a third party for scanning. The email is then sent back (via SMTP) to the original receiving domain, which may consider the incoming email as a newly seen message. This is sometimes seen in federal agencies that use one provider for email and another provider for Trusted Internet Connection (TIC) services (see Figure 4-2). Incoming mail is received by the cloud provider, then forwarded to the TIC provider for scanning. After scanning, the email message is sent back to the cloud provider. Upon the second delivery, the message appears to be spoofed, as SPF and DMARC validations will fail.

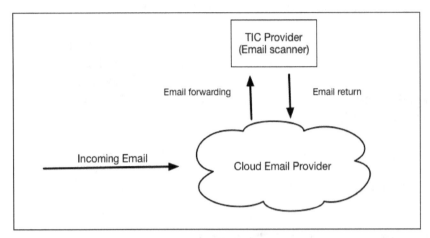

Figure 4-3: Use of Cloud Email with Third Party Email Scanning

Table 4-7 below summarizes the various forwarding techniques and their effect on domain-based authentication mechanisms:

Table 4-7: Common relay techniques and their impact on domain-based authentication

Relay Technique	Typical Uses	Negatively Impacts
Aliases	Forwarding, many-to-one consolidation, vanity addresses	SPF
Re-sender	MUA level forwarding, inline forwarding	SPF & DKIM
Mailing Lists	Re-posting to a subscriber list, often with modifications to the message body (such as a footer identifying the mailing list).	SPF & DKIM results may lead to DMARC policy rejection and sender unsubscribe
Gateways	Unrestricted message re-writing, and forwarding	SPF & DKIM
Boundary Filters	Spam or malware filters that change/delete content of an email message	DKIM
Third Parties	Email malware scanners, TIC providers	SPF & DMARC

One solution that can reduce the impact due to domain-based validation failures is the Authenticated Receiver Chain (ARC)[14] extension. ARC is an extension of DKIM that generates a chain of custody (called an "ARC Set") as an email message moves from one MTA to another. The ARC Set is actually three new headers that contain a receiver's authentication results, an additional signature over the message a second signature over selected headers (including the other ARC headers). Downstream receivers include their authentication results as well as also signing the previous handler's ARC headers. ARC can be used to give information about authentication results throughout the chain of possession. ARC is not perfect because a malicious actor can alter the ARC Set, so ARC should only be seen as a purported chain of custody and a way to use indirect email flows without invalidating previous authentication results.

ARC may be especially useful when using third party email scanners (or TIC providers). A federal agency's cloud email provider can forward all email to the TIC provider for scanning. Upon resubmission of the email, the cloud email provider can examine the ARC chain to see that the incoming email was validated previously and only returning from (known) third party scanning and override the sending domain's DMARC policy in favor of a local policy about messages received from the TIC provider that has a valid ARC chain. As of the time of writing, ARC is still being finalized in the IETF. However, email service providers and administrators are encouraged to look at ARC as a means to minimize the impact of domain-based validation failures when forwarding email, or when using email mailing lists.

Forwarding in general creates problems for DMARC results processing, and as of this writing, universal solutions are still in development. There is a currently existing set of mitigations that could be used by the mail relay and by the receiver, but would require modified MTA processing from traditional SPF and DKIM processing:

1. The mediator can alter the message-From: field to match the envelope-From:. In this case the SPF lookup would be on the mediator's domain.
2. After making the customary modifications, which break the originators DKIM signature, the email relay can generate its own DKIM signature over the modified header and body. Multiple DKIM signatures in a message are acceptable and DMARC policy is that at least one of the signatures must authenticate to pass DMARC.

It should also be noted that if one or the other (SPF or DKIM) authentication and domain alignment checks pass, then the DMARC policy could be satisfied.

At the receiver side, if a message fails DMARC and is bounced (most likely in the case where the sender publishes a **p=reject** policy), then a mailing list may respond by unsubscribing the recipient. Mailing list managers should be sensitive to the reasons for rejection and avoid unsubscribing recipients if the bounce is due to message authentication issues. If the mailing list is in a domain where the recommendations in this document can be applied, then such mailing

---

[14] Authenticated Receiver Chain (ARC) Protocol. Work-in-Progress. https://datatracker.ietf.org/doc/draft-ietf-dmarc-arc-protocol/

list managers should be sensitive to and accommodate DMARC authentication issues. In the case where the mailing list is outside the domain of influence, the onus is on senders and receivers to mitigate the effects of forwarding as best they can. ARC may also be useful in mitigating these types of errors, as a receiver can examine the ARC chain for additional information about how the message traveled through different MTAs.

4.7   Authenticating Mail Messages with Digital Signatures

In addition to authenticating the sender of a message, the message contents can be authenticating with digital signatures. Signed email messages protect against phishing attacks, especially targeted phishing attacks, as users who have been conditioned to expect signed messages from co-workers and organizations are likely to be suspicious if they receive unsigned messages instructing them to perform an unexpected action [GAR2005]. For this reason, the Department of Defense requires that all e-mails containing a hyperlink or an attachment be digitally signed [DOD2009].

Because it interoperates with existing PKI and most deployed software, S/MIME is the recommended format for digitally signing messages. Users of most email clients who receive S/MIME signed messages from organizations that use well-known CAs will observe that the message signatures are automatically validated, without the need to manually add or trust certificates for each sender. If users receive mail that originates from a sender that uses a non-public CA, then either the non-public CA must be added or else each S/MIME sender must be individually approved. Today, the US Government PIV [FIPS 201] cards are signed by well-known CAs, whereas the US Department of Defense uses CAs that are generally not trusted outside the Department of Defense. Thus, email signed by PIV cards will generally be validated with no further action, while email signed by DoD Common Access Cards will result in a warning that the sender's certificate is not trusted.

4.7.1 End-to-End Authentication Using S/MIME Digital Signatures

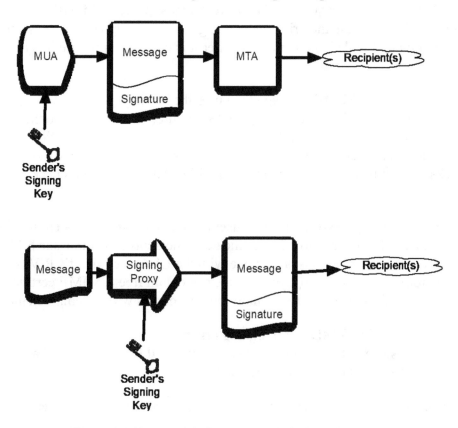

Figure 4-4: Two models for sending digitally signed mail.

Organizations (and individuals in organizations) can use S/MIME digital signatures to certify email that is sent within or external to the organization. Because support for S/MIME is present in many modern mail clients[15], S/MIME messages that are signed with a valid digital signature will automatically validate when they are displayed. This is particularly useful for messages that are designed to be read but not replied to—for example, status reports and alerts that are sent programmatically, as well as messages that are sent to announcement-only distribution lists.

To send S/MIME digitally signed messages, organizations must first obtain a S/MIME certificate where the sender matches the message-From: address that will be used to sign the messages. Typically, this will be done with a S/MIME certificate and matching private key that corresponds to the role, rather than to an individual.[16] Once a certificate is obtained, the message is first composed. Next, software uses both the S/MIME certificate and the private portion of their S/MIME key pair to generate the digital signature. S/MIME signatures contain both the signature and the signing certificate, allowing recipients to verify the signed message without having to

---

[15] Support for S/MIME is included in Microsoft Outlook, Apple Mail, iOS Mail, Mozilla Thunderbird, and other mail programs.
[16] For example, DoDI 8520.02 (May 24, 2011), "Public Key Infrastructure (PKI) and Public Key (PK) Enabling," specifically allows certificates to be issued for groups, roles, information system, device, and code signing purposes, in addition to the issuance of certificates to eligible users.

fetch the certificate from a remote server; the certificate itself is validated using PKI. Sending S/MIME signed messages thus requires either a MUA that supports S/MIME and the necessary cryptographic libraries to access the private key and generate the signature, or else an intermediate program that will sign the message after it is created but before it is delivered (Fig 4-3).

The receiver of the signed S/MIME message then uses the sender's public key (from the sender's attached X.509 certificate) and validates the digital signature. The receiver should also check to see if the senders certificate has a valid PKIX chain back to a root certificate the receiver trusts to further authenticate the sender. Some organizations may wish to configure MUAs to perform real-time checks for certificate revocation and an additional authentication check (See Section 5.2.2.3).

The principal barrier to using S/MIME for end-user digital signatures has been the difficulty of arranging for end-users to obtain S/MIME certificates. One approach is to issue S/MIME credentials in physical identity tokens, as is done with the US Government's PIV (Personal Identity Verification) cards [FIPS 201]. Individuals can obtain free S/MIME certificates from a number of online providers, who verify the individual's address with an email challenge.

The principal barrier to using S/MIME for signing organizational email has been the lack of attention to the issue, since only a single certificate is required for signing mail and software for verifying S/MIME signatures is already distributed.

Security Recommendation 4-11: Use S/MIME signatures for assuring message authenticity and integrity.

4.8   Recommendation Summary

Security Recommendation 4-1: Organizations are recommended to deploy SPF to specify which IP addresses are authorized to transmit email on behalf of the domain. Domains controlled by an organization that are not used to send email, for example Web only domains, should include an SPF RR with the policy indicating that there are no valid email senders for the given domain.

Security Recommendation 4-2: Organizations should deploy DNSSEC for all DNS name servers and validate DNSSEC responses from all systems that receive email.

Security Recommendation 4-3: Federal agency administrators shall only use keys with approved algorithms and lengths for use with DKIM.

Security Recommendation 4-4: Administrators should ensure that the private portion of the key pair is adequately protected on the sending MTA and that only the MTA software has read privileges for the key. Federal agency administrators should follow FISMA control SC-12 [SP800-53] guidance with regards to distributing and protecting DKIM key pairs.

Security Recommendation 4-5: Each sending MTA should be configured with its own private key and its own selector value, to minimize the damage that may occur if a private key is compromised.

Security Recommendation 4-6: Organizations should deploy DNSSEC to provide authentication and integrity protection to the DKIM DNS resource records.

Security Recommendation 4-7: Organizations should enable DNSSEC validation on DNS servers used by MTAs that verify DKIM signatures.

Security Recommendation 4-8: Mailing list software should verify DKIM signatures on incoming mail and re-sign outgoing mail with new DKIM signatures.

Security Recommendation 4-9: Mail sent to broadcast mailing lists from do-not-reply or unmonitored mailboxes should be digitally signed with S/MIME signatures so that recipients can verify the authenticity of the messages.

Security Recommendation 4-10: A unique DKIM key pair should be used for each third party that sends email on the organization's behalf.

Security Recommendation 4-11: Use S/MIME signatures for assuring message authenticity and integrity.

5   Protecting Email Confidentiality

5.1   Introduction

Cleartext mail messages are submitted by a sender, transmitted hop-by-hop over a series of relays and delivered to a receiver. Any successful man-in-the-middle can intercept such traffic and read it directly. Any bad actor, or organizationally privileged actor, can read such mail on the submission or delivery systems. Email transmission security can be assured by encrypting the traffic along the path. The Transport Layer Security protocol (TLS) [RFC5246] protects confidentiality by encrypting bidirectional traffic and prevents passive monitoring. TLS relies on public key cryptography and uses X.509 certificates [RFC5280] to encapsulate the public key, and the Certificate Authority (CA) system to issue certificates and authenticate the origin of the key.

In recent years the CA system has become the subject of attack and has been successfully compromised on several occasions.[17][18] The DANE protocol [RFC6698] is designed to overcome problems in the CA system by providing an alternative channel for authenticating public keys using DNSSEC. The result is that the same trust relationships used to certify IP addresses can be used to certify servers operating on those addresses the mechanisms that combine to improve the assurance of email transmission security are described in section 5.2.

Encryption at the transport layer gives assurance of the integrity of data in transit, but senders and receivers who want end-to-end assurance, (i.e., mailbox to mailbox) of confidentiality have two alternative mechanisms for achieving this: S/MIME [RFC5750] and OpenPGP [RFC4880]. Both protocols are capable of signing (for authentication) and encryption (for confidentiality). The S/MIME protocol is deployed to sign and/or encrypt message contents, using keys stored as X.509 certificates and a PKI (See Section 2.4.2) while OpenPGP uses a different certificate and a Web-of-Trust model for authentication of identities (See Section 2.4.3). Both of these protocols have the issue of trustworthy certificate publication and discovery. Traditionally, this was done using dedicated key/certificate servers, LDAP servers, etc., but these methods are not always easy to deploy and standardize for every enterprise. These certificates can be published through the DNS by a different implementation of the DANE mechanism for S/MIME [RFC8162] and OpenPGP [RFC7929]. S/MIME and OpenPGP, with their strengthening by DANE authentication are discussed below.

5.2   Email Transmission Security

Email proceeds towards its destination from a Message Submission Agent (MSA), through a sequence of Message Transfer Agents (MTAs), to a Message Delivery Agent (MDA), as described in Section 2. This translates to the use of SMTP [RFC5321] for submission and hop-by-hop transmission and IMAP [RFC3501] or POP3 [RFC1939] for final delivery into a

---

[17] "Comodo SSL Affiliate The Recent RA Compromise," Phillip Hallam Baker, Comodo, March 15, 2011.
    https://blog.comodo.com/other/the-recent-ra-compromise/
[18] Peter Bright, "Independent Iranian hacker claims responsibility for Comodo hack," Ars Technica, March 28, 2011.
    http://arstechnica.com/security/2011/03/independent-iranian-hacker-claims-responsibility-for-comodo-hack/

recipient's mailbox. TLS [RFC5246] can be used to protect email in transit for one or more hops, but intervening hops may be under autonomous control, so a securely encrypted end-to-end path cannot be guaranteed. This is discussed further in section 5.2.1. Opportunistic encryption over some portions of the path can provide "better-than-nothing" security. The use of STARTTLS [RFC3207] is a standard method for establishing a TLS connection. TLS has a secure handshake that relies on asymmetric encryption, to establish a secure session (using symmetric encryption). As part of the handshake, the server sends the client an X.509 certificate containing its public key, and the cipher suite and symmetric key are negotiated with a preference for the optimally strongest cipher that both parties support. SMTP clients have traditionally not verified the server's certificate due to the lack of an appropriate mechanism to specify allowable certificates and certificate authorities. The newly adopted RFC 7672 [RFC 7672] rectifies this, by providing rules for applying the DANE protocol to SMTP servers. The use of DANE in conjunction with SMTP is discussed Section 5.2.4.

Ultimately the entire path from sender to receiver will be protected by TLS. But this may consist of many hops between MTAs, each the subject of a separate transport connection. These are not compelled to upgrade to TLS at the same time, however in the patchwork evolutionary development of the global mail system, this cannot be completely guaranteed. There may be some MTAs along the route uncontrolled by the sender or receiver domains that have not upgraded to TLS. In the interim until all mail nodes are certifiably secure, the principle is that some incrementally improving security is better than no security, so opportunistic TLS (using DANE or other methods to validate certificates) should be employed at every possible hop.

5.2.1   TLS Configuration and Use

Traditionally, sending email begins by opening an SMTP connection over TCP and entering a series of cleartext commands, possibly even including usernames and passwords. This leaves the connection exposed to potential monitoring, spoofing, and various man-in-the-middle interventions. A clear improvement would be to open a secure connection that is encrypted so that the message contents cannot be passively monitored, and third parties cannot spoof message headers or contents. Transport Layer Security (TLS) offers the solution to these problems.

TCP provides a reliable, flow-controlled connection for transmitting data between two peers. Unfortunately, TCP provides no built-in security. Transport connections carry all manner of sensitive traffic, including web pages with financial and sign-in information, as well as email messages. This traffic can only be secured through physical isolation, which is not possible on the Internet, or by encrypting the traffic.

The Secure Sockets Layer (SSL) was developed to provide a standard protocol for encrypting TCP connections. SSL evolved into Transport Layer Security (TLS), the most recent version at the time of writing being Version 1.3 [RFC8446]. TLS negotiates a secure connection between initiator and responder (typically client and server) parties. The negotiation entails the exchange of the server's certificate, and possibly the client's certificate, and agreement on a cipher to use for encrypting the data. In essence, the protocol uses the public-private key pair: the public key in the server's certificate, and the server's closely held private key, to negotiate a symmetric algorithm and establish a key known to both parties, and with which both can encrypt, transmit and decrypt the application data. RFC 5246 Appendix A describes a range of permissible ciphers, and the parties agree on one from this set. This range of ciphers may be restricted on some hosts by local policy (such as only ciphers Approved for federal use). Data transmitted over the connection is encrypted using the negotiated session key. At the end, the connection is closed, and the session key can be deleted (but not always, see below).

Negotiating a TLS connection involves a significant time and processor load, so when the two parties have the need to establish frequent secure connections between them, a session resumption mechanism allows them to continue with the previously negotiated cipher, for a subsequent connection.

TLS gains its security from the fact that the server holds the private key securely and the public key can be authenticated due to it being wrapped in an X.509 certificate that is guaranteed by some Certificate Authority. If the Certificate Authority is somehow compromised, there is no guarantee that the key in the certificate is truly the one belonging to the server, and a client may inadvertently negotiate with a man-in-the-middle. An investigation of what X.509 certificates are, how they work, and how they can be better secured, follows.

Security Recommendation 5-1: Organizations are recommended only use approved TLS versions listed in NIST SP 800-52 [SP800-52] with FIPS approved cryptographic modules.

5.2.2 X.509 Certificates

The idea of certificates as a secure and traceable vehicle for locating a public key, its ownership and use was first proposed by the Consultative Committee for International Telephony and Telegraphy (CCITT), now the International Telecommunications Union (ITU). The X.509 specification was developed and brought into worldwide use as a result. In order to vest a certificate with some authority, a set of Certificate Authorities is licensed around the world as identifiable authentic sources. Each certificate hierarchy has a traceable root for authentication and has specific traceable requirements for revocation if that is necessary. As a certificate has a complex set of fields, the idea of a certificate profile has more recently come into play. X.509 certificate formats are described in Section 5.2.2.1, their authentication in Section 5.2.2.2, and possible revocation in Section 5.2.2.3. The profile concept and a specific example are described in Section 5.2.2.4

5.2.2.1 X.509 Description

A trusted Certificate Authority (CA) is licensed to validate applicants' credentials, store each applicant's public key in a X.509 [RFC5280] structure, and digitally sign it with the CA's private key. Each applicant must first generate their own public and private key pair, save the private key securely, and wrap the public key into an X.509 request. The **openssl req** command is an example of how to do this on Unix/Linux systems with OpenSSL[19] installed. Many CAs will generate a certificate without receiving a request (in effect, generating the request themselves on

---

[19] https://www.openssl.org/

the customer's behalf). The resulting digitally encoded structure is transmitted to the CA, vetted according to the CA's policy, and a certificate is issued. An example certificate is given below in Figure 5-1, with salient fields described.

- **Issuer:** The Certificate Authority that issued and signed this end-entity certificate. If the issuer is a well-known reputable entity, its root certificate may be listed in host systems' root certificate repository.
- **Subject:** Sometimes referred to as the common name (CN). The entity to which this certificate is issued by this CA. Here: **www.example.com**.
- **Public Key:** (this field truncated for readability). This is the public key corresponding to the private key held by the subject. Clients who receive the certificate in a secure communication attempt extract the public key and use it for one of the stated key usages.
- **X509v3 Key Usage:** The use of this certificate is restricted to digital signature, key encipherment or key agreement. So an attempt to use it for data encipherment, for example, should result in error.
- **X509v3 Basic Constraints:** This certificate is an end certificate so the constraint is set to **CA:FALSE**. It is not a CA certificate and its key cannot be used to sign downstream certificates for other entities.
- **X509v3 SubjectAltName:** Together with the common name in the Subject field, this represents the binding of the public key to a domain. Any attempt by another domain to transmit this certificate to try to establish a connection should result in failure to authenticate and connection closure by the client.
- **Signature Algorithm** (truncated for convenience). The signature generated by the CA over this certificate, demonstrating the CA's authentication of the subject and its public key.

```
Certificate:
    Data:
        Version: 3 (0x2)
        Serial Number: 760462 (0xb9a8e)
    Signature Algorithm: sha1WithRSAEncryption
        Issuer: C=IL, O=ExampleCA LLC, OU=Secure Digital Certificate Signing, CN=ExampleCA Primary
Intermediate Server CA
        Validity
            Not Before: Aug 20 15:32:55 2013 GMT
            Not After : Aug 21 10:17:18 2014 GMT
        Subject: description=l0Yrz4bhzFN7q1lb, C=US,
CN=www.example.com/emailAddress=admin@example.com
        Subject Public Key Info:
            Public Key Algorithm: rsaEncryption
                Public-Key: (2048 bit)
                Modulus:
                    00:b7:14:03:3b:87:aa:ea:36:3b:b2:1c:19:e3:a7:
                    7d:84:5b:1e:77:a2:44:c8:28:b7:c2:27:14:ef:b5:
                    04:67
                Exponent: 65537 (0x10001)
```

```
X509v3 extensions:
    X509v3 Basic Constraints:
        CA:FALSE
    X509v3 Key Usage:
        Digital Signature, Key Encipherment, Key Agreement
    X509v3 Extended Key Usage:
        TLS Web Server Authentication
    X509v3 Subject Key Identifier:
        C2:64:A8:A0:3B:E6:6A:D5:99:36:C2:70:9B:24:32:CF:77:46:28:BD
    X509v3 Authority Key Identifier:
        keyid:EB:42:34:D0:98:B0:AB:9F:F4:1B:6B:08:F7:CC:64:2E:EF:0E:
2C:45
    X509v3 Subject Alternative Name:
        DNS:www.example.com, DNS:example.com
    X509v3 Certificate Policies:
        Policy: 2.23.140.1.2.1
        Policy: 1.3.6.1.4.1.23223.1.2.3
          CPS: http://www.exampleCA.com/policy.txt
          User Notice:
            Organization: ExampleCA Certification Authority
            Number: 1
            Explicit Text: This certificate was issued according to the Class 1 Validation requirements of
the ExampleCA CA policy, reliance only for the intended purpose in compliance of the relying party
obligations.

    X509v3 CRL Distribution Points:
        Full Name:
          URI:http://crl.exampleCA.com/crl.crl

    Authority Information Access:
        OCSP - URI:http://ocsp.exampleCA.com/class1/server/ocsp
        CA Issuers - URI:http://aia.exampleCA.com/certs/ca.crt

    X509v3 Issuer Alternative Name:
        URI:http://www.exampleCA.com/
Signature Algorithm: sha1WithRSAEncryption
    93:29:d1:ed:3a:2a:91:50:b4:64:1d:0f:06:8a:79:cf:d5:35:
    ba:25:39:b0:dd:c0:34:d2:7f:b3:04:5c:46:50:2b:97:72:15:
    ea:3a:4f:b6
```

Figure 5-1: Example of X.509 Certificate

5.2.2.2 X.509 Authentication

The certificate given above is an example of an end certificate. Although it claims to be signed by a well-known CA, anyone receiving this certificate in communication has the problem of authenticating that signature. For this, full PKIX authentication back to the root certificate is required. The CA issues a well-known self-signed certificate containing its public key. This is the root certificate. A set of current root certificates, often numbering in the hundreds of certificates, are held by individual browser developers and operating system suppliers as their set of trusted root certificates. The process of authentication is the process of tracing the end certificate back to a root certificate, through a chain of zero or more intermediate certificates.

5.2.2.3 Certificate Revocation

Every certificate has a period of validity typically ranging from 30 days up to a number of years. There may, however, be reasons to revoke a certificate prior to its expiration, such as the compromise or loss of the private key [RFC5280]. The act of revocation is associated with the CA publishing a certificate revocation list. Part of authenticating a certificate chain is perusing the certificate revocation list (CRL) to determine if any certificate in the chain is no longer valid. The presence of a revoked certificate in the chain should result in failure of authentication. Among the problems of CRL management, the lack of real-time revocation checks leads to non-determinism in the authentication mechanism. Problems with revocation led the IETF to develop a real-time revocation management protocol, the Online Certificate Status Protocol (OCSP) [RFC6960]. Mozilla has now taken the step to deprecate CRLs in favor of OCSP.

5.2.2.4 Certificate Profiles

The Federal Public Key Infrastructure (FPKI) Policy Authority has specified profiles (called the FPIX profile) for two types of X.509 version 3 certificates that can be used for confidentiality and integrity protection of federal email systems [FPKI-CERT]. The applicable certificate profile is identified by the **KeyPurposeId** with value **id-kp-emailProtection (1.3.6.1.5.5.7.3.4)** and includes the following:

- End-Entity Signature Certificate Profile (Worksheet 5)
- Key Management Certificate Profile (Worksheet 6)

The overall FPIX profile is an instantiation of IETF's PKI profile developed by the PKIX working group (and hence called the PKIX profile) [PKIX] with unique parameter settings for Federal PKI systems. Thus, a FPIX certificate profile complements the corresponding PKIX certificate profile. The following is a brief overview of the two applicable FPIX profiles referenced above.

5.2.2.4.1 Overview of Key Management Certificate Profile

The public key of a Key Management certificate is used by a device (e.g., a Mail Transfer Agent (MTA) in this context) to set up a session key (a symmetric key) with its transacting entity (e.g., the next-hop MTA in this context). The parameter values specified in the profile for this certificate type, for some of the important fields are:

- **Signature**: (of the certificate issuer) If the RSA is used as the signature algorithm for signing the certificate by the CA, then the corresponding hash algorithms can only be either SHA-256 or SHA-512.
- **subjectPublicKeyInfo**: The allowed algorithms for the public key are RSA, Diffie-Hellman (DH), Elliptic Curve (ECC), or the Key Exchange Algorithm (KEA).
- **KeyUsage**: The keyEncipherment bit is set to 1 when the subject public key is RSA. The KeyAgreement bit is set to 1 when the subject public key is Diffie-Hellman (DH), Elliptic Curve (ECC), or Key Exchange Algorithm (KEA).

- **KeyPurposeId**: Should include the value **id-kp-emailProtection (1.3.6.1.5.5.7.3.4)**
- **subjectAltName**: Since this certificate is used by devices (as opposed to a human subject), this field should contain the DNS name or IP Address.

5.2.3 STARTTLS

Unlike the World Wide Web, where the URL indicates that the secure variant (i.e., HTTPS) is in use, an email sender has only the email address, "**user@domain**", to signal the destination and no way to direct that the channel must be secured. This is an issue not just on a sender-to-receiver basis, but also on a transitive basis, as SMTP is not an end-to-end protocol but instead a protocol that sends mail messages as a series of hops (i.e., MUA, MSA, multiple MTAs, etc.). Not only is there no way to signal that message submission must be secure, there is also no way to signal that any hop in the transmission should be secure. STARTTLS was developed to address some of the shortcomings of this system.

RFC 3207 [RFC3207] describes an extension to SMTP that allows an SMTP client and server to use TLS to provide private, authenticated communication across the Internet. This gives SMTP agents the ability to protect some or all of their communications from eavesdroppers and attackers. If the client initiates the connection over a TLS-enabled port (e.g., port 465 was previously used for SMTP over SSL), the server advertises that the STARTTLS option is available to connecting clients. The client can then issue the STARTTLS command in the SMTP command stream, and the two parties proceed to establish a secure TLS connection. An advantage of using STARTTLS is that the server can offer SMTP service on a single port, rather than requiring separate port numbers for secure and cleartext operations. Similar mechanisms are available for running TLS over IMAP and POP protocols.

When STARTTLS is initiated as a request by the server side, it may be susceptible to a downgrade attack, where a man-in-the-middle (MITM) is in place. In this case the MITM receives the STARTTLS request from the server reply to a connection request and scrubs it out. The initiating client sees no TLS upgrade request and proceeds with an unsecured connection (as originally anticipated). Likewise, most MTAs default to sending messages over unencrypted TCP if certificate validation fails during the TLS handshake.

Domains can signal their desire to receive email over TLS by publishing a public key in their DNS records using DANE (Section 5.2.4). Domains can also configure their email servers to reject mail that is delivered without being preceded by a TLS upgrade. Unfortunately, doing so at the present time may result in email not being delivered from clients that are not capable of TLS. Furthermore, mail that is sent over TLS will still be susceptible to MITM attacks unless the client verifies the that the server's certificate matches the certificate that is advertised using DANE.

If the client wants to ensure an encrypted channel, there is a new proposal to allow for signaling the required use of TLS via the REQUIRETLS SMTP option[20]. This option is set by senders to indicate that they wish TLS to be used for each hop and not deliver to the next hop if TLS is not available. If the server wishes to indicate that an encrypted channel is available and should be used by senders, this can be indicated through an advertisement using DANE. If the end user wants security over the message content, then the message should be encrypted using S/MIME or OpenPGP, as discussed in Section 5.3.

In this long transition period towards "TLS everywhere," there will be security gaps where some MTA to MTA hop offers TCP only. In these cases, the receiving MTA suggestion of STARTTLS can be downgraded by the above MITM attack. In such cases, a channel thought secure by the end user can be compromised. A mitigating consolation is that opportunistic security (i.e., use encryption when available) is better than no security. The more mail administrators who actively deploy TLS, the fewer opportunities for effective MITM attacks. In this way global email security improves incrementally.

5.2.3.1 Recommendations

Security Recommendation 5-2: TLS-capable servers should prompt clients to invoke the STARTTLS command. TLS clients should attempt to use STARTTLS for SMTP, either initially, or issuing the command when offered.

5.2.4 SMTP Security via Opportunistic DNS-based Authentication of Named Entities (DANE) Transport Layer Security (TLS)

For years, TLS has solved the problem of distributing public keys by using a certificate, signed by some well-known Certification Authority (CA). Every browser developer and operating system supplier maintain a list of CA root certificates as trust-anchors. These are called the software's *root certificates* and are stored in the *root certificate store*. The PKIX procedure allows the certificate recipient to trace a certificate back to the root. So long as the root certificate remains trustworthy, and the authentication concludes successfully, the client can proceed with the connection.

Currently, there are hundreds of organizations acting as CAs on the Internet. If one CA infrastructure or vetting procedure is compromised, the attacker can obtain the CA's private key, or get issued certificates under a false name. There is no limitation of scope for the global PKI, and a compromise of a single CA damages the integrity of the entire PKI system.

Aside from a CA compromise, some CAs have engaged in poor security practices. For example, some CAs have issued wildcard certificates that allow the holder to issue sub-certificates for any domain or entity, anywhere in the world.[21]

---

[20] J. Fenton *SMTP Require TLS Option*. Work in Progress https://datatracker.ietf.org/doc/draft-ietf-uta-smtp-require-tls/

[21] For examples of poor CA issuing practices involving sub-certificates, see "Bug 724929—Remove Trustwave Certificate(s)

DANE introduces mechanisms for domains to specify to a client which certificates should be trusted for the domain. With DANE, a domain owner can publish DNS records that declare clients should only trust certificates from a particular CA or that they should only trust only a specific certificate or public key. Essentially, DANE replaces reliance on the security provided by the CA system with reliance on the security provided by DNSSEC.

DANE complements TLS. The TLS handshake yields an encrypted connection between a server and a client and provides a server's X.509 certificate to the client.[22] The TLS protocol does not define how the certificate should be authenticated. Some implementations may do this as part of the TLS handshake, and some may leave it to the application to perform authentication. Whichever way is used, there is still a vulnerability: a CA can issue certificates for any domain, and if that a CA is compromised (as has happened more than once all too recently), an attacker can have it can issue a replacement certificate for any domain and take control of a server's connections. Ideally, issuance and delivery of a certificate should be tied absolutely to the given domain. DANE creates this explicit link by allowing the server domain owner to create a TLSA resource record in the DNS [RFC6698] [RFC7671], which identifies the certificate, its public key, or a hash of either. When the client receives an X.509 certificate in the TLS negotiation, it looks up the TLSA RR for that domain and matches the TLSA data against the certificate as part of the client's certificate validation procedure.

DANE has a number of usage models (called Certificate Usages) to accommodate users who require different forms of authentication. These Certificate Usages are given mnemonic names [RFC7218]:

- With Certificate Usage DANE-TA(2), the TLSA RR designates a trust-anchor that issued one of the certificates in the PKIX chain. [RFC7671] requires that DANE-TA(2) trust anchors be included in the server "certificate message" unless the entire certificate is specified in the TLSA record (i.e., usage 2 0 0, indicating the TLSA RR contains a local root certificate).

- With Certificate Usage DANE-EE(3), the TLSA RR matches an end-entity, or leaf certificate.

- Certificate Usages PKIX-TA(0) and PKIX-EE(1) should not be used for opportunistic DANE TLS encryption [RFC 7672]. This is because, outside of web browsers, there is no authoritative list of trusted certificate authorities, and PKIX-TA(0) and PKIX-EE(1) require that both the client and the server have a prearranged list of mutually trusted CAs.

In DANE-EE(3) the server certificate is directly specified by the TLSA record. Thus, the

---

from trusted root certificates," February 7, 2012. https://bugzilla.mozilla.org/show_bug.cgi?id=724929, Also "Bug 698753—Entrust SubCA: 512-bit key issuance and other CPS violations; malware in wild," November 8, 2011. https://bugzilla.mozilla.org/show_bug.cgi?id=698753. Also "Revoking Trust in one CNNIC Intermediate Certificate," Mozilla Security Blog, March 23, 2015. https://blog.mozilla.org/security/2015/03/23/revoking-trust-in-one-cnnic-intermediate-certificate/.

[22] Also possibly from client to server.

certificate may be self-issued, or it may be issued by a well-known CA. The certificate may be current or expired. Indeed, operators may employ either a public or a private CA for their DANE certificates and publish a combination of "3 1 1" and "2 1 1" TLSA records, both of which should match the server chain and be monitored. This allows clients to verify the certificate using either DANE or the traditional Certificate Authority system, significantly improving reliability.

Secure SMTP communications involves additional complications because of the use of mail exchanger (MX) and canonical name (CNAME) DNS RRs, which may cause mail to be routed through intermediate hosts or to final destinations that reside at different domain names. [RFC 7671] and [RFC7672] describe a set of rules that are to be used for finding and interpreting DANE policy statements.

As originally defined, TLS did not offer a client the ability to specify a particular hostname when connecting to a server; this was a problem in the case where the server offers multiple virtual hosts from one IP address, and there was a desire to associate a single certificate with a single hostname. [RFC6066] defines a set of extensions to TLS that include the Server Name Indication (SNI), allowing a client to specifically reference the desired server by hostname, and the server can respond with the correct certificate.

[RFC7671] and [RFC7672] require the client to send SNI just in case the server needs this to select the correct certificate. There is no obligation on the server to employ virtual hosting, or to return a certificate that matches the client's SNI extension. There is no obligation on the client to match anything against the SNI extension. Rather, the requirement on the client is to support at least the TLSA base domain as a reference identifier for the peer identity when performing name checks (matching against a TLSA record other than DANE-EE(3)). With CNAME expansion either as part of MX record resolution or address resolution of the MX exchange, additional names must be supported as described in [RFC7671] and [RFC7672].

A DANE matching condition also requires that the connecting server match the SubjectAltName from the delivered end certificate to the certificate indicated in the TLSA RR. DANE-EE authentication allows for the server to deliver a self-signed certificate. In effect, DANE-EE is simply a vehicle for delivering the public key. Authentication is inherent in the trust provided by DNSSEC, and the SNI check is not required.

5.2.5   SMTP MTA Strict Transport Security (MTA-STS)

Some email providers regard the requirement that DANE records be secured with DNSSEC as a major barrier to deployment. As an alternative, they have proposed SMTP Strict Transport Security [RFC8461], which relies on records that are announced via DNS but authenticated using information distributed via HTTPS. The goal of MTA-STS is the same as DANE: to have a way for a receiving MTA to publish its TLS policy and mitigate Man-in-the-Middle (MITM) spoofing. SMA-STS can be used with DANE, as neither method precludes the use of the other.

MTA-STS works by publishing both a special TXT RR in the DNS and a policy document at a Well-Known URL. The client obtains both artifacts before attempting to establish a connection to the receiving domain's mail servers.

66

5.2.5.1 The MTA-STS DNS Resource Record

The receiving domain administrator generates an MTA-STS policy RR (a TXT Text RR) with the following tag:value pairs (separated by ";"):

Table 5-1: MTA-STS Resource Record Tags and Descriptions

Tag	Descriptions
v=	Version of MTA-STS in use. Currently, the only defined value is **STSv1**
id=	A string used to indicate policy instance. Used to signal to clients that the receiver's policy has changed. It must be changed every time there is a policy update on the receiver's side.

The MTA-STS RR is published as a TXT RR using the receiving domain with **_mta-sts** prepended. For example, if the receiving domain is **example.gov**, the MTA-STS RR is:

_mta-sts.example.gov   IN   TXT   "v=STSv1; id=20170101000000Z"

5.2.5.2 The MTA-STS Policy

The receiver then published a detailed policy document at a well-known URL consisting of the domain with **mta-sts** prepended and **.well-known/mta-sts.txt** as the path. So, in the example above, the URL containing the MTA-STS policy for **example.gov** would be found at:

https://mta-sts.example.gov/.well-known/mta-sts.txt

The policy must only be accessible via HTTPS and contains a plain/text resource used by the client to connect to the receiver. The document contains tag:values pairs, separated by newlines. The tags are:

Table 5-2: MTA-STS Policy Tags and Descriptions

Tag	Description
version:	The version of MTA-STS in use by the receiver. Currently, the only defined value is **STSv1**
mode:	The requested behavior of clients if a TLS validation failure or MX matching failure occurs. Defined values are **enforce**, meaning a client should reject the connection, **report**, meaning a client should stop the connection and send a TLS failure report (see Section XX) and **none**, meaning a client should continue with the connection.
mx:	A hostname of a mail receiver that should be present (as common name or subject alternative name) in any received X.509 server certificates sent during a TLS handshake. A receiver's policy resource may contain multiple **mx=** tags, each on a separate line.
max_age:	Maximum lifetime of a policy (in seconds). Used as a time to live for a cached policy. Clients should recheck the receiver's MTA-STS URL for a possible updated policy after the **max_age** has elapsed.

An example MTA-STS policy for **example.gov** may look like the following (found at the URL above):

```
version: STSv1
mode: enforce
mx: mail1.example.gov.
mx: mail2.example.gov.
max_age:86400
```

In the above, **example.gov** lists two mail servers for the domain (**mail1.example.gov** and **mail2.example.gov**). The domain also sets its policy to enforce, meaning that if a client sees a server certificate that lacks **mail1.example.gov** or **mail2.example.gov**, or encounters some other PKIX validation failure, it is to reject the connection.

An MTA-STS compliant sender first checks for the presence of an MTA-STS policy at the receiver domain. First by checking its cache to see if an earlier discovered policy was found, or by looking in the DNS for the MTA-STS DNS RR. If it is a newly discovered policy, the client first gets the policy over HTTPS, then attempts to connect to each candidate MX listed in order in the policy. For each receiving mail server, the sender attempts to connect via STARTTLS, and validates the receiver's server certificate. If successful, the message is delivered. If not, the sender moves on to the next mail server listed in the policy. If none of the connections are successful, the sender does not deliver the message.

At the time of writing, there are no publicly available MTA-STS implementations, and only a single MTA-STS Internet draft has been posted. Therefore, it is not possible for organizations to deploy MTA-STS aware clients at the present time.

5.2.6 Comparing DANE and MTA-STS

Both DANE and MTA-STS were designed to assist opportunistic encryption and combat passive monitoring of SMTP connections. Receiving domains can support both if desired, to support all clients. Senders can implement both as well, as the current MTA-STS spec states that DANE DNSSEC responses take precedence. The basic merits of both are summarized in the table below:

Table 5-3: Comparing DANE and MTA-STS

Feature	DANE	MTA-STS
DNS RRType used	TLSA RRs	TXT RRs
Client Requirements	DNSSEC	HTTPS
CA scoping?	Yes	No
PKIX required?	No always	Yes
Self-Signed certificates acceptable?	Yes (when using CU=3)	No
Failure reporting to receiver?	No	Yes
Client behavior on failure	Close connection	Depends on policy

Security Recommendation 5-3: Receiving domains should implement protocols to signal TLS usage to clients. Receivers should implement DANE, MTA-STS (or both) for all mail servers listed in the domain's MX Resource Record set.

Security Recommendation 5-4: As federal agency use requires certificate chain authentication against a known CA, Certificate Usage DANE-TA(2) is recommended when deploying DANE to specify the CA that the agency has chosen to employ. Agencies should also publish a DANE-EE(3) RR alongside the DANE-TA(2) RR for increased reliability. In both cases the TLSA record should use a selector of SPKI(1) and a Matching field type of SHA2-256(1), for parameter values of "3 1 1" and "2 1 1" respectively.

5.2.7 Reporting TLS Errors to Senders

Currently, there is no way for an MTA to report TLS failures to a receiving domain. If a sending MTA cannot establish a TLS protected connection, there is no automated signaling to the receiver as to the nature of the failure, only the receiver's own logs. Previously, most MTAs would simply continue to connect without TLS and deliver the mail. However, with options such as MTA-STS (Section 5.2.5) or REQUIRETLS (Section 5.2.3), TLS errors will cause more failures in delivery.

There is a way to have a standard way to report TLS failures back to receivers known as SMTP TLS Reporting [RFC8460]. The concept is similar to DMARC (see Section 4.6) where receivers send failure reports back to senders, only here senders send the failure report. The specification includes the report format as well as how to signal reporting over SMTP or HTTPS. HTTPS is given as an option for senders that wish to use a secure channel but believe SMTP over TLS will not work. Also, like DMARC, the location (via email or HTTPS) where reports should be sent are published in a DNS TXT resource record that the sender can query for in the receiver's domain. Here the TXT RR has a well-known string **_smtp.-tls** prepended and using the following tag:value pairs each separated by a semicolon ';':

Table 5-4: TLS Reporting Value Tags and Descriptions

Tag	Description
v=	The version string. Default is **TLSRPTv1**
rua=	How the receiver wishes to have reports submitted. Options are **mailto:** (for email) or **https** (for a URI to submit reports via a POST command).

An example TLS reporting RR is given below for **example.gov**:

_smtp-tlsrpt.example.gov IN TXT
    "v=TLSRPTv1;rua=https://reporttls.example.gov/reports"

Indicating that TLS failure reports when connecting to **example.gov** mail receivers should be sent to the URI listed in the **rua** tag. A reporting RR may have multiple values in the **rua** tag, indicating several alternative means to send reports.

5.3 Email Content Security

End users and their institutions have an interest in rendering the contents of their messages completely secure against unauthorized eyes. They can take direct control over message content security using either S/MIME [RFC5751] or OpenPGP [RFC4880]. In each of these protocols, the sender signs a message with a private key, and the receiver authenticates the signature with the public key obtained (somehow) from the sender. Signing provides a guarantee of the message source, but any man in the middle can use the public key to decode and read the signed message. For proof against unwanted readers, the sender encrypts a message with the recipient's public key or with a generated symmetric key that is encrypted with the receiver's public key which is obtained (somehow) from the receiver. The receiver decrypts the message with the corresponding private key, or a symmetric key encrypted with the recipient's public key, and the message content is kept confidential from mailbox to mailbox. Both S/MIME and OpenPGP are protocols that facilitate signing and encryption, but secure open distribution of public keys is still a hurdle. Two recent DANE protocols have been proposed to address this. The SMIMEA (for S/MIME certificates) and OPENPGPKEY (for OpenPGP keys) initiatives specify new DNS RR types for storing email end user key material in the DNS. S/MIME and SMIMEA are described in subsection 5.3.1, while OpenPGP and OPENPGPKEY are described in subsection 5.3.2.

5.3.1 S/MIME and SMIMEA

S/MIME is a protocol that allows email users to authenticate messages by digitally signing with a private key and including the public key in an attached certificate. The recipient of the message performs a PKIX validation on the certificate, authenticating the message's originator. On the encryption side, the S/MIME sender typically encrypts the message text using a generated symmetric key, which is encrypted in turn with the public key of the recipient, which was previously distributed using some other, out of band, method. Within an organization it is common to obtain a correspondent's S/MIME certificate from an LDAP directory server. Another way to obtain a S/MIME certificate is by exchanging digitally signed messages.

S/MIME had the advantage of being based on X.509 certificates, allowing existing software and procedures developed for the PKI to be used for email. Hence, where the domain-owning enterprise has an interest in securing the message content, S/MIME is preferred.

The Secure/Multipurpose Internet Mail Extensions (S/MIME) [RFC5751] describes a protocol that will sign, encrypt or compress some, or all, of the body contents of a message. Signing is done using the sender's private key, while key encipherment is done with the recipient's known public key. Message encryption using the data encryption key, signing and compression can be done in any order and any combination. The operation is applied to the body, not the RFC 5322 headings of the message. In the signing case, the certificate containing the sender's public key is also attached to the message.

The receiver uses the associated public key to authenticate the digital signature over the message, demonstrating proof of origin and non-repudiation. The usual case is for the receiver to authenticate the supplied certificate using PKIX back to the Certificate Authority. Users who want more assurance that the key supplied is bound to the sender's domain can deploy the SMIMEA mechanism [RFC8162] in which the certificate and key can be independently retrieved from the DNS and authenticated per the DANE mechanism, similar to that described in Sub-section 5.2.5, above. The user who wants to encrypt a message retrieves the receiver's public key: which may have been sent on a prior signed message[23]. If no prior signed message is at hand, or if the user seeks more authentication than PKIX, then the key can be retrieved from the DNS in an SMIMEA record. The receiver decrypts the data encryption key using the corresponding private key, decrypts the message using the newly decrypted key and reads or stores the message as appropriate.

---

[23] The use of one key pair for both digital signatures and data encryption is not recommended, but very common.

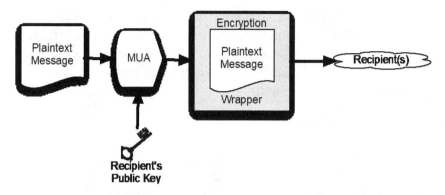

Figure 5-2: Sending an Encrypted Email

To send an S/MIME encrypted message (Fig 2-4) to a user, the sender must first obtain the recipient's X.509 certificate and may (optionally) validate the certificate to a trusted root, if possible. The sender then uses the certificate's public key to generate a data encryption key and use that generated key to encrypt the composed message. In this case the sender must possess the recipient's certificate before sending the message.

An enterprise looking to use S/MIME to provide email confidentiality will need to obtain or produce credentials for each end user in the organization. An organization can generate its own root certificate and give its members a certificate generated from that root, or purchase certificates for each member from a well-known Certificate Authority (CA).

Using S/MIME for end-user encryption is further complicated by the need to distribute each end-users' certificate to potential senders. Traditionally this is done by having correspondents exchange email messages that are digitally signed that includes the sender's encryption certificate, but not encrypted. Alternatively, organizations can configure LDAP servers to make S/MIME public keys available as part of a directory lookup; mail clients such as Outlook and Apple Mail can be configured to query LDAP servers for public keys necessary for message encryption.

5.3.1.1 S/MIME Recommendations

Official use requires certificate chain authentication against a known Certificate Authority.

Current MUAs use S/MIME private keys to decrypt the data encryption key that was used to encrypt the email message each time that it is displayed, but leave the message encrypted in the email store. This mode of operation is not recommended, as it forces the recipient of the encrypted email to maintain their private key indefinitely. Instead, the email should be decrypted prior to being stored in the mail store. The mail store, in turn, should be secured using an appropriate cryptographic technique (for example, disk encryption), extending protection to both encrypted and unencrypted email. If it is necessary to store mail encrypted on the mail server (for example, if the mail server is outside the control of the end-user's organization), then the messages should be re-encrypted with a changeable session key on a message-by-message basis.

Where the DNS performs canonicalization of email addresses, a client requesting a hash encoded OPENPGPKEY or SMIMEA RR shall perform no transformation on the left part of the address offered, other than UTF-8 and lower-casing. This is an attempt to minimize the queries needed to discover an S/MIME certificate in the DNS for newly learned email addresses and allow for the initial email to be sent encrypted (if desired).

5.3.2 OpenPGP and OPENPGPKEY

OpenPGP [RFC4880] is a proposed Internet Standard for providing authentication and confidentiality for email messages. Although similar in purpose to S/MIME, OpenPGP is distinguished by using message and key formats that are built on the "Web of Trust" model (see Section 2.4.3).

The OpenPGP standard is implemented by PGP-branded software from Symantec[24] and by the open source GNU Privacy Guard.[25] These OpenPGP programs have been widely used by activists and security professionals for many years but have never gained a widespread following among the general population owing to usability programs associated with installing the software, generating keys, obtaining the keys of correspondents, encrypting messages, and decrypting messages. Academic studies have found that even "easy-to-use" versions of the software that received good reviews in the technical media for usability were found to be not usable when tested by ordinary computer users. [WHITTEN1999]

Key distribution was an early usability problem that OpenPGP developers attempted to address. Initial efforts for secure key distribution involved *key distribution parties*, where all participants are known to and can authenticate each other. This method does a good job of authenticating users to each other and building up webs of trust, but it does not scale at all well, and it is not greatly useful where communicants are geographically widely separated.

To facilitate the distribution of public keys, a number of publicly available key servers have been set up and have been in operation for many years. Among the more popular of these is the pool of SKS key servers[26]. Users can freely upload public keys on an opportunistic basis. In theory, anyone wishing to send a PGP user encrypted content can retrieve that user's public key from the SKS server, use it to encrypt a generated data encryption key used to encrypt the message, and send it. However, there is no authentication of the identity of the key owners; an attacker can upload their own key to the key server, then intercept the email sent to the unsuspecting user.

A renewed interest in personal control over email authentication and encryption has led to further work within the IETF on key sharing, and the DANE mechanism [RFC7929] is being adopted to place a domain and user's public key in an OPENPGPKEY record in the DNS. Unlike DANE/TLS and SMIMEA, OPENPGPKEY does not use X.509 certificates, or require full PKIX authentication as an option. Instead, full trust is placed in the DNS records as certified by DNSSEC: The domain owner publishes a public key and minimal "certificate" information. The

---

[24] http://www.symantec.com/products-solutions/families/?fid=encryption
[25] https://www.gnupg.org/
[26] An incomplete list of well-known keyservers can be found at https://www.sks-keyservers.net

key is available for the receiver of a signed message to authenticate, or for the sender of a message to encrypt a data encryption key.

Security Recommendation 5-5: For Federal use, OpenPGP is not preferred for message confidentiality. The use of S/MIME with a certificate signed by a known CA is preferred.

5.3.2.1 Recommendations

Where an institution requires signing and encryption of end-to-end email, S/MIME is preferred over OpenPGP. Like the S/MIME discussion above, if used, the email should be decrypted prior to being stored in the mail store. The mail store, in turn, should be secured using an appropriate cryptographic technique (for example, disk encryption), extending protection to both encrypted and unencrypted email. If it is necessary to store mail encrypted on the mail server (for example, if the mail server is outside the control of the end-user's organization), then the messages should be re-encrypted with a changeable session key on a message-by-message basis. In addition, where the DNS performs canonicalization of email addresses, a client requesting a hash encoded OPENPGPKEY or SMIMEA RR shall perform no transformation on the left part of the address offered, other than UTF-8 and lower-casing.

5.4 Security Recommendation Summary

Security Recommendation 5-1: Organizations are recommended only use approved TLS versions listed in NIST SP 800-52 with FIPS approved cryptographic modules.

Security Recommendation 5-2: TLS-capable servers should prompt clients to invoke the STARTTLS command. TLS clients should attempt to use STARTTL for SMTP, either initially, or issuing the command when offered.

Security Recommendation 5-3: Receiving domains should implement protocols to signal TLS usage to clients. Receivers should implement DANE, MTA-STS (or both) for all mail servers listed in the domain's MX Resource Record set.

Security Recommendation 5-4: Official use of digitally signed/encrypted email requires certificate chain authentication against a known CA and using DANE-TA Certificate Usage values when deploying DANE.

Security Recommendation 5-5: Do not use OpenPGP for message confidentiality. Instead, use S/MIME with a certificate that is signed by a known CA.

6   Reducing Unsolicited Bulk Email

6.1   Introduction

Unsolicited Bulk Email (UBE) has an analogy with "beauty", in that it is often in the eye of the beholder. To some senders, it is a low-cost marketing campaign for a valid product or service. To many receivers and administrators, it is a scourge that fills up message inboxes and can be a vector for criminal activity or malware. Both of these views can be true, as the term Unsolicited Bulk Email (or *spam*, as it is often called) comprises a wide variety of email received by an enterprise.

6.2   Why an Organization May Want to Reduce Unsolicited Bulk Email

While some unsolicited email is from legitimate marketing firms and may only rise to the level of being a nuisance, it can also lead to increased resource usage in the enterprise. UBE can fill up user inbox storage, consume bandwidth in receiving email and consume end users' time as they sort through and delete unwanted email. However, some UBE may rise to the level of being a legitimate threat to the organization in the form of fraud, illegal activity, or the distribution of malware.

Depending on the organization's jurisdiction, UBE may include advertisements for goods or services that are illegal. Enterprises or organizations may wish to limit their employees' (and users') exposure to these offers. Other illegitimate UBE are fraud attempts aimed at the users of a given domain and used to obtain money or private information. Lastly, some UBE is simply a Trojan horse aimed at trying to infiltrate the enterprise to install malware.

6.3   Techniques to Reduce Unsolicited Bulk Email

There are a variety of techniques that an email administrator can use to reduce the amount of UBE delivered to the end users' inboxes. Enterprises can use one or multiple technologies to provide a layered defense against UBE since no solution is completely effective against all UBE. Administrators should consider using a combination of tools for processing incoming, and outgoing email.

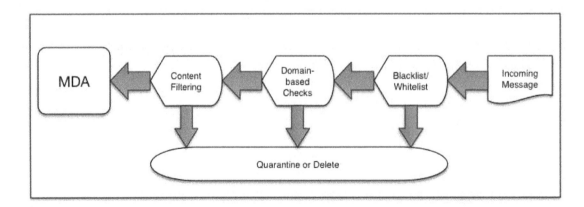

Figure 6-1: Inbound email "pipeline" for UBE filtering

These techniques can be performed in serial as a "pipeline" for both incoming and outgoing email [REFARCH]. Less computationally expensive checks should be done early in the pipeline to prevent wasted effort later. For example, a UBE/SMTP connection that would be caught and refused by a blacklist filter should be done before more computationally expensive content analysis is performed on an email that will ultimately be rejected or deleted. In Figure 6-1, an example pipeline for incoming email checks is given. Figure 6-2 shows an example outbound pipeline for email checks.

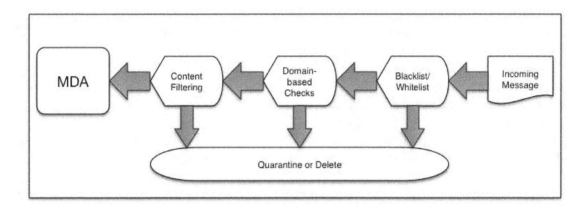

Figure 6-2: Outbound email "pipeline" for UBE filtering

6.3.1   Approved/Non-approved Sender Lists

The most basic technique to reduce UBE is to simply accept or deny messages based on some list of known bad or known trusted senders. This is often the first line of UBE defense utilized by an enterprise because, if a message was received from a known bad sender, it could reasonably be dropped without spending resources in further processing. Or, email originating from a trusted source could be marked so as not to be subject to other anti-UBE checks and inadvertently deleted or thrown out.

A *non-approved sender list* can be composed of individual IP addresses, IP blocks, or sending domain bases [RFC5782]. For example, it is normal for enterprises to refuse email from senders using a source address that has not be allocated, or part of a block reserved for private use (such as 192.168/16). Or an administrator could choose to not accept email from a given domain if there is no reason to assume that they have any interaction with senders using a given domain. This could be the case where an organization does not do business with certain countries and may refuse mail from senders using those country code Top Level Domains (ccTLDs).

Given the changing nature of malicious UBE, static lists are not effective. Instead, a variety of third party services produce dynamic lists of known bad UBE senders that enterprise administrators can subscribe to and use. These lists are typically accessed by DNS queries and include the non-commercial ventures such as the Spamhaus Project[27] and the Spam and Open

---

[27] https://www.spamhaus.org/

Relay Blocking System (SORBS)[28], as well as commercial vendors such as SpamCop.[29] An extensive list of DNS-based blacklists can be found at http://www.dnsbl.info. Because an individual service may be unavailable, many organizations configure their mailers to use multiple blacklists. Email administrators should use these services to maintain a dynamic reject list rather than attempting to maintain a static list for a single organization.

An *approved list* is the opposite of a non-approved list. Instead of refusing email from a list of known bad actors, an approved list is composed of known trusted senders. It is often a list of business partners, community members, or similar trusted senders that have an existing relationship with the organization or members of the organization. This does not mean that all email sent by members on an approved list should be accepted without further checks. Email sent by an approved sender may not be subject to other anti-UBE checks but may still be checked for possible malware or malicious links. Email administrators wishing to use approved list should be very stringent about which senders make the list. Frequent reviews of the list should also occur to remove senders when the relationship ends or add new members when new relationships are formed. Some email tools allow for end users to create their own approved list, so administrators should make sure that end users do not approve a known bad sender.

A list of approved/non-approved receivers can also be constructed for outgoing email to identify possible victims of malicious UBE messages or infected hosts sending UBE as part of a botnet. That is, a host or end user sending email to a domain or setting the message-From: address domain to one listed in a non-approved receiver list. Again, since this is a relatively easy (computational) activity, it should be done before any more intensive scanning tools are used.

6.3.2   Domain-based Authentication Techniques

Techniques that use sending policy encoded in the DNS, such as Sender Policy Framework (SPF), DomainKeys Identified Mail (DKIM), and Domain-based Message Authentication and Reporting Conformance (DMARC) can also be used to reduce some UBE. Receiving MTAs use these protocols to see if a message was sent by an authorized sending MTA for the purported domain. These protocols are discussed in Section 4 and should be utilized by email administrators for both sending and receiving email.

These protocols only authenticate that an email was sent by a mail server that is considered a valid email sender by the purported domain and does not authenticated the contents of the email message. Messages that pass these checks should not automatically be assumed to not be UBE, as a malicious bulk email sender can easily set up and use their own sending infrastructure that would pass these checks. Likewise, malicious code that uses an end user's legitimate account to send email will also pass domain-based authentication checks.

Domain-based authentication checks require more processing by the receiver MTA and thus should be performed on any mail that has passed the first set of blacklist checks. These checks do

---

[28] http://www.sorbs.net/
[29] https://www.spamcop.net/

not require the MTA to have the full message and can be done before any further and more computationally expensive content checks.[30]

6.3.3 Content Filtering

The third type of UBE filtering measures involves analysis of the actual contents of an email message. These filtering techniques examine the content of a mail message for words, phrases or other elements (images, web links, etc.) that indicate that the message may be UBE.

Examining the textual content of an email message is done using word/phrase filters or Bayesian filters [UBE1] to identify possible UBE. Since these techniques are not foolproof, most tools that use these techniques allow for administrators or end users to set the threshold for UBE identification or allow messages to be marked as possible UBE to prevent false positives and the deletion of valid transactional messages.

Messages that contain URLs or other non-text elements (or attachments) can also be filtered and tested for possible malware, UBE advertisements, etc. This could be done via blacklisting (blocking email containing links to known malicious sites) or by opening the links in a sandboxed browser-like component[31] in an automated fashion to record the results. If the activity corresponds to anomalous or known malicious activity, the message will be tagged as malicious UBE and deleted before placed into the end-user's in-box.

Content filtering and URL analysis is more computationally expensive than other UBE filtering techniques since the checks are done over the message contents. This means that the checks are often done after blacklisting and domain-based authentication checks have completed. This avoids accepting and processing email from a known bad or malicious sender. End-to-end encryption of messages (e.g., S/MIME or OpenPGP) can also prevent content filtering.

Content filtering could also be applied to outgoing email to identify possible botnet infection or malicious code attempting to use systems within the enterprise to send UBE. Some content filters may include organization-specific filters or keywords to prevent the loss of private or confidential information.

6.4 User Education

The final line of defense against malicious UBE is an educated end user. An email user that is aware of the risks inherent in using email should be less likely to fall victim to fraud attempts, social engineering or convinced into clicking links containing malware. While such training may not stop all suspicious email, often times an educated end user can sometimes detect and avoid malicious UBE that passes all automated checks.

---

[30] Messages are transmitted incrementally with SMTP, header by header and then body contents and attachments. This allows for incremental and 'just-in-time' header and content filtering.

[31] Sometimes called a "detonation chamber."

How to setup a training regime that includes end user education on the risks of UBE to the enterprise is beyond the scope of this document. There are several federal programs to help in end user IT security training, such as the "Stop. Think. Connect."[32] program from the Department of Homeland Security (DHS). Individual organizations should tailor available IT security education programs to the needs of their organization.

User education does not fit into the pipeline model in Section 6.3 above, as it takes place at the time that the end user views the email using their MUA. At this point, all of the above techniques have failed to identify the threat that now has been placed in the end user's in-box. For outgoing UBE, the threat is being sent out (possibly using the user's email account) via malicious code installed on the end user's system. User education can help to prevent users from allowing their machines to become infected with malicious code or teach them to identify and remediate the issue when it arises.

---

[32] https://www.dhs.gov/stopthinkconnect

7   End User Email Security

7.1   Introduction

In terms of the canonical email processing architecture as described in Section 2, the client may play the role of the MUA. This section we will discuss clients and their interactions and constraints when using POP3, IMAP, and SMTP. The range of an end user's interactions with a mailbox is usually done using one of two classes of clients: webmail clients and standalone clients. These clients communicate with the mailbox in different ways. Webmail clients use HTTPS. These are discussed in Section 7.2. Mail client applications for desktop or mobile devices may use IMAP or POP3 for receiving and SMTP for sending, and these are examined in Section 7.3. There is also the case of command-line clients, the original email clients that are still used for certain embedded system accesses. However, these represent no significant proportion of the enterprise market and will not be discussed in this document.

7.2   Webmail Clients

Many enterprises permit email access while away from the workplace or the corporate LAN. The mechanisms for this access is a Virtual Private Network (VPN) or a web interface through a browser. In the latter case, the security posture is determined at the web server. Actual communication between a client and server is conducted over HTTP or HTTPS. Federal agencies implementing a web-based solution should refer to NIST SP 800-95 [SP800-95] and adhere to other federal policies regarding web-based services. Federal agencies are required to provide a certificate that can be authenticated through PKIX to a well-known trust-anchor. An enterprise may choose to retain control of its own trusted roots. In this case, DANE can be used to configure a TLSA record and authenticate the certificate using the DNS (see Section 5.2.5).

7.3   Standalone Clients

For the purposes of this guide, a *standalone client* refers to a software component used by an end user to send and/or receive email. Examples of such clients include Mozilla Thunderbird and Microsoft Outlook. These components are typically found on a host computer, laptop or mobile device. These components may have many features beyond basic email processing, but these are beyond the scope of this document.

Sending requires connecting to an MSA or an MTA using SMTP. This is discussed in Section 7.3.2. Receiving is typically done via POP3 and IMAP,[33] and mailbox management differs in each case.

7.3.1   Sending via SMTP

Email message submission occurs between a client and a server using the Simple Mail Transfer Protocol (SMTP) [RFC5321], either using port 25, 465 or 587. The client is operated by an end-

---

[33] Other protocols (MAPI/RPC or proprietary protocols) will not be discussed.

user, and the server is hosted by a public or corporate mail service. Clients should authenticate using client authentication schemes such as usernames and passwords or PKI-based authentication as provided by the protocol.

It is further recommended that the connection between the client and MSA be secured using TLS [RFC5246] [RFC8314], associated with the full range of protective measures described in Section 5.2.

7.3.2 Receiving via IMAP

Email message receiving, and management occurs between a client and a server using the Internet Message Access Protocol (IMAP) protocol [RFC3501] over port 143 and 993. A client may be located anywhere on the Internet, establish a transport connection with the server, authenticate itself, and manipulate the remote mailbox with a variety of commands. Depending on the server implementation, it is feasible to have access to the same mailbox from multiple clients. IMAP has operations for creating, deleting and renaming mailboxes; checking for new messages; permanently removing messages; parsing; searching; and selective fetching of message attributes, texts and parts thereof. It is equivalent to the local control of a mailbox and its folders.

Establishing a connection with the server over TCP and authenticating to a mailbox with a username and password sent without encryption is not recommended. IMAP clients should connect to servers using TLS [RFC5246] [RFC8314], which should be associated with the full range of applicable protective measures described in Section 5.2.

7.3.3 Receiving via POP3

Before IMAP [RFC3501] was invented, the Post Office Protocol (POP, now POP version 3 or POP3) had been created as a mechanism for remote users to connect to mailbox, download mail, and delete it off the server. It was expected at the time that access be from a single, dedicated user, with no conflicts. Provision for encrypted transport was not made.

The protocol went through an evolutionary cycle of upgrades, and the current instance, POP3 [RFC5034] is aligned with the Simple Authentication Security Layer (SASL) [RFC4422] and optionally operated over a secure encrypted transport layer, TLS [RFC5246]. POP3 defines a simpler mailbox access alternative to IMAP, without the same fine control over mailbox file structure and manipulation mechanisms. Users who access their mailboxes from multiple hosts or devices should use IMAP clients instead of POP3, to maintain a synchronization of clients with the single, central mailbox.

Clients with POP3 access should configure them to connect over TLS [RFC8314], which should be associated with the full range of protective measures described above in Section 5.2, Email Transmission Security.

Security Recommendation 7-1: IMAP and POP3 clients should connect to servers using TLS [RFC5246] and be associated with the full range of protective measures described in

Section 5.2, Email Transmission Security. Connecting with unencrypted TCP and authenticating with username and password is strongly discouraged.

7.4   Mailbox Security

The security of data in transit is only useful if the security of data at rest can be assured. This means maintaining confidentiality at the sender and receiver endpoints of:

- The user's information (e.g., mailbox contents), and
- Private keys.

Confidentiality and the encryption for data in transit is discussed in Section 7.4.1, while the confidentiality of data at rest is discussed in Section 7.4.2.

7.4.1   Confidentiality of Data in Transit

A common element for users of TLS for SMTP, IMAP and POP3, as well as for S/MIME and OpenPGP, is the need to maintain current and accessible private keys, as used for decryption of received mail, and signing of authenticated mail. A range of different users require access to these disparate private keys:

- The email server must have use of the private key used for TLS and the private key must be protected.
- The end user (and possibly an enterprise security administrator) must have access to private keys for S/MIME or OpenPGP message signing and key decipherment.

Special care is needed to ensure that only the relevant parties have access and control over the respective keys. For federal agencies, this means compliance with all relevant policy and best practice for the protection of key material [SP800-57pt1] and message contents (e.g., FOIA, eDiscovery, etc.).

Security Consideration 7-2: Enterprises should establish a cryptographic key management system (CKMS) for keys associated with protecting email sessions with end users. For federal agencies, this means compliance with all relevant policy and best practice for the protection of key material [SP800-57pt1].

7.4.2   Confidentiality of Data at Rest

This publication is about securing email and its associated data. This is one aspect of securing data in transit. To the extent that email comes to rest in persistent storage in mailboxes and file stores, there is some overlap with NIST SP 800-111 [SP800-111].

There is an issue in the tradeoff between accessibility and confidentiality when using mailboxes as persistent storage. End users and their organizations are expected to manage their own private keys, and historical versions of these may remain available to enable the decryption of mail encrypted by communicating partners, and to authenticate cc: mail sent to partners, which have been also stored locally. Partners who sign their mail, and decrypt received mail, make their public keys available through certificates, or through DANE records (i.e., TLSA, OPENPGPKEY, SMIMEA) in the DNS. These certificates generally have a listed expiry date and are rolled over and replaced with new certificates containing new keys. For people who use their mailboxes as persistent, large-scale storage, this can create a management problem. If a mail user's expired keys cannot be found, historical encrypted messages cannot be read.

Email keys for S/MIME and OpenPGP should only be used for messages in transit. Messages intended for persistent local storage should be decrypted, stored in user-controllable file storage, and, if necessary, re-encrypted with user-controlled keys. For maximum security, all email should be stored encrypted—for example, with a cryptographic file system.

Security Recommendation 7-3: Cryptographic keys used for encrypting data in persistent storage (e.g., in mailboxes) should be different from keys used for the transmission of email messages.

7.5   Security Recommendation Summary

Security Recommendation 7-1: IMAP and POP3 clients should connect to servers using TLS [RFC5246] and be associated with the full range of protective measures described in Section 5.2, Email Transmission Security. Connecting with unencrypted TCP and authenticating with username and password is strongly discouraged.

Security Consideration 7-2: Enterprises should establish a cryptographic key management system (CKMS) for keys associated with protecting email sessions with end users. For federal agencies, this means compliance with all relevant policy and best practice for the protection of key material [SP800-57pt1].

Security Recommendation 7-3: Cryptographic keys used for encrypting data in persistent storage (e.g., in mailboxes) should be different from keys used for the transmission of email messages.

Appendix A—Acronyms

Selected acronyms and abbreviations used in this paper are defined below.

DHS	Department of Homeland Security
DKIM	DomainKeys Identified Mail
DMARC	Domain-based Message Authentication, Reporting and Conformance
DNS	Domain Name System
DNSSEC	Domain Name System Security Extensions
FISMA	Federal Information Security Management Act
FRN	Federal Network Resiliency
IMAP	Internet Message Access Protocol
MDA	Mail Delivery Agent
MSA	Mail Submission Agent
MTA	Mail Transport Agent
MUA	Mail User Agent
MIME	Multipurpose Internet Message Extensions
NIST SP	NIST Special Publication
PGP/OpenPGP	Pretty Good Privacy
PKI	Public Key Infrastructure
POP3	Post Office Protocol, Version 3
RR	Resource Record
S/MIME	Secure/Multipurpose Internet Mail Extensions
SMTP	Simple Mail Transport Protocol
SPF	Sender Policy Framework
TLS	Transport Layer Security
VM	Virtual Machine
VPN	Virtual Private Network

Appendix B—References

B.1   NIST Publications

[FIPS 201]   Federal Information Processing Standards Publication 201-2: *Personal Identity Verification (PIV) of Federal Employees and Contractors*. National Institute of Standards and Technology, Gaithersburg, Maryland, August 2013. https://doi.org/10.6028/NIST.FIPS.201-2

[SP800-45]   NIST Special Publication 800-45 version 2. *Guidelines on Electronic Mail Security*. National Institute of Standards and Technology, Gaithersburg, Maryland, February 2007. https://doi.org/10.6028/NIST.SP.800-45ver2

[SP800-52]   NIST Special Publication 800-52 Revision 1. *Guidelines for the Selection, Configuration, and Use of Transport Layer Security (TLS) Implementations*. National Institute of Standards and Technology, Gaithersburg, Maryland, April 2014. https://doi.org/10.6028/NIST.SP.800-52r1

[SP800-53]   NIST Special Publication 800-53 Revision 4. *Security and Privacy Controls for Federal Information Systems and Organizations*. National Institute of Standards and Technology, Gaithersburg, Maryland, April 2013. https://doi.org/10.6028/NIST.SP.800-53r4

[SP800-57pt1]   NIST Special Publication 800-57 Part 1 Revision 4. *Recommendation for Key Management, Part 1: General*. National Institute of Standards and Technology, Gaithersburg, Maryland, January 2016. https://doi.org/10.6028/NIST.SP.800-57pt1r4

[SP800-57pt3]   NIST Special Publication 800-57 Part 3 Revision 1. *Recommendation for Key Management, Part 3: Application-Specific Key Management Guidance*. National Institute of Standards and Technology, Gaithersburg, Maryland, January 2015. https://doi.org/10.6028/NIST.SP.800-57pt3r1

[SP800-81]   NIST Special Publication 800-81 Revision 2, *Secure Domain Name System (DNS) Deployment Guide,* National Institute of Standards and Technology, Gaithersburg, Maryland, September 2013. https://doi.org/10.6028/NIST.SP.800-81-2

[SP800-95]   NIST Special Publication 800-95. *Guide to Secure Web Services*. National Institute of Standards and Technology, Gaithersburg, Maryland, August 2007. https://doi.org/10.6028/NIST.SP.800-95

[SP800-111]   NIST Special Publication 800-111. *Guide to Storage Encryption Technologies for End User Devices*. National Institute of Standards and Technology, Gaithersburg, Maryland, November 2007. https://doi.org/10.6028/NIST.SP.800-111

[SP800-130]   NIST Special Publication 800-130. *A Framework for Designing Cryptographic Key Management Systems*. National Institute of Standards and Technology, Gaithersburg, Maryland, August 2013. https://doi.org/10.6028/NIST.SP.800-130

[SP800-152]   NIST Special Publication 800-152. *A Profile for U.S. Federal Cryptographic Key Management Systems (CKMS)*. National Institute of Standards and Technology, Gaithersburg, Maryland, October 2015. https://doi.org/10.6028/NIST.SP.800-152

B.2   Core Email Protocols

[RFC2045]   N. Freed and N. Borenstein. *Multipurpose Internet Mail Extensions (MIME) Part One: Format of Internet Message Bodies*. Internet Engineering Task Force Request for Comments 2045, November 1996. https://datatracker.ietf.org/doc/rfc2045/

[RFC2046]   N. Freed and N. Borenstein. *Multipurpose Internet Mail Extensions (MIME) Part Two: Media Types* Internet Engineering Task Force Request for Comments 2046, November 1996. https://datatracker.ietf.org/doc/rfc2046/

[RFC2047]   N. Freed and N. Borenstein. *Multipurpose Internet Mail Extensions (MIME) Part Three: Message Headers for Non-ASCII Text* Internet Engineering Task Force Request for Comments 2047, November 1996. https://datatracker.ietf.org/doc/rfc2047/

[RFC2822]   P. Resnick. *Internet Message Format*. Internet Engineering Task Force Request for Comments 2822, April 2001. https://datatracker.ietf.org/doc/rfc2822/

[RFC3501]   M. Crispin. *INTERNET MESSAGE ACCESS PROTOCOL - VERSION 4rev1*. Internet Engineering Task Force Request for Comments 3501, March 2003. https://datatracker.ietf.org/doc/rfc3501/

[RFC3696]   J. Klensin. Application Techniques for Checking and Transformation of Names. Internet Engineering Task Force Request for Comments 3696, February 2004. https://datatracker.ietf.org/doc/rfc3696/

[RFC5321]   J. Klensin. *Simple Mail Transfer Protocol*. Internet Engineering Task Force Request for Comments 5321, April 2008. https://datatracker.ietf.org/doc/rfc5321/

[RFC5322]   P. Resnick. *Internet Message Format*. Internet Engineering Task Force Request for Comments 5322, October 2008.

https://datatracker.ietf.org/doc/rfc5322/

[RFC7601]   M. Kucherawy. *Message Header Field for Indicating Message Authentication Status*. Internet Engineering Task Force Request for Comments 7601, August 2015. https://datatracker.ietf.org/doc/rfc7601/

[RFC8314]   K. Moore and C. Newman. *Cleartext Considered Obsolete: Use of Transport Layer Security (TLS) for Email Submission and Access*. Internet Engineering Task Force Request for Comments 8314, August 2015. https://datatracker.ietf.org/doc/rfc8314/

[STD35]   J. Myers and M. Rose. *Post Office Protocol - Version 3*. Internet Engineering Task Force Standard 35. May 1996. https://datatracker.ietf.org/doc/rfc1939/

B.3   Sender Policy Framework (SPF)

[HERZBERG   Amir Herzberg. 2009. DNS-based email sender authentication mechanisms:
2009]   A critical review. *Computer. Security*. 28, 8 (November 2009), 731-742. https://doi.org/10.1016/j.cose.2009.05.002

[RFC7208]   S. Kitterman. *Sender Policy Framework (SPF) for Authorizing Use of Domains in Email, Version 1*. Internet Engineering Task Force Request for Comments 7208, April 2014. https://datatracker.ietf.org/doc/rfc7208/

B.4   DomainKeys Identified Mail (DKIM)

[RFC4686]   J. Fenton. *Analysis of Threats Motivating DomainKeys Identified Mail (DKIM)*. Internet Engineering Task Force Request for Comments 4686, September 2006. https://datatracker.ietf.org/doc/rfc4686/

[RFC5863]   T. Hansen, E. Siegel, P. Hallam-Baker and D. Crocker. *DomainKeys Identified Mail (DKIM) Development, Deployment, and Operations*. Internet Engineering Task Force Request for Comments 5863, May 2010. https://datatracker.ietf.org/doc/rfc5863/

[RFC6376]   D. Cocker, T. Hansen, M. Kucherawy. *DomainKeys Identified Mail (DKIM) Signatures*. Internet Engineering Task Force Request for Comments 6376, September 2011. https://datatracker.ietf.org/doc/rfc6376/

[RFC6377]   M. Kucherawy. *DomainKeys Identified Mail (DKIM) and Mailing Lists*. Internet Engineering Task Force Request for Comments 6377, September 2011. https://datatracker.ietf.org/doc/rfc6377/

[RFC8463]   J. Levine. *A New Cryptographic Signature Method for DomainKeys Identified Mail (DKIM)*. Internet Engineering Task Force Request for Comments 8463, September 2018. https://datatracker.ietf.org/doc/rfc8463/

B.5   Domain-based Message Authentication, Reporting and Conformance (DMARC)

[RFC6591]   H. Fontana. *Authentication Failure Reporting Using the Abuse Reporting Format*. Internet Engineering Task Force Request for Comments 6591, November 2007. https://datatracker.ietf.org/doc/rfc6591/

[RFC7489]   M. Kucherawy and E. Zwicky. *Domain-based Message Authentication, Reporting, and Conformance (DMARC)*. Internet Engineering Task Force Request for Comments 7489, March 2015. https://datatracker.ietf.org/doc/rfc7489/

B.6   Cryptography and Public Key Infrastructure (PKI)

[RFC3207]   P. Hoffman. *SMTP Service Extension for Secure SMTP over Transport Layer Security*. Internet Engineering Task Force Request for Comments 3207, February 2002. https://datatracker.ietf.org/doc/rfc3207/

[RFC3156]   M. Elkins, D. Del Torto, R. Levien and T. Roessler. *MIME Security with OpenPGP*. Internet Engineering Task Force Request for Comments 3156, August 2001. https://datatracker.ietf.org/doc/rfc3156/

[RFC4422]   A. Melnikov and K. Zeilenga. *Simple Authentication and Security Layer (SASL)*. Internet Engineering Task Force Request for Comments 4422, June 2006. https://datatracker.ietf.org/doc/rfc4422/

[RFC4880]   J. Callas, L. Donnerhacke, H. Finney, D. Shaw and R. Thayer. *OpenPGP Message Format*. Internet Engineering Task Force Request for Comments 4880, November 2007. https://datatracker.ietf.org/doc/rfc4880/

[RFC5034]   R. Siemborski and A. Menon-Sen. *The Post Office Protocol (POP3) Simple Authentication and Security Layer (SASL) Authentication Mechanism*. Internet Engineering Task Force Request for Comments 5034, July 2007. https://datatracker.ietf.org/doc/rfc5034/

[RFC5091]   X. Boyen and L. Martin. *Identity-Based Cryptography Standard (IBCS) #1: Supersingular Curve Implementations of the BF and BB1 Cryptosystems* Internet Engineering Task Force Request for Comments 5091, December

2007. https://datatracker.ietf.org/doc/rfc5091/

[RFC5280]   D. Cooper, S. Santesson, S. Farrell, S. Boeyen, R. Housley, and W. Polk. *Internet X.509 Public Key Infrastructure Certificate and Certificate Revocation List (CRL) Profile.* Internet Engineering Task Force Request for Comments 5280, May 2008. https://datatracker.ietf.org/doc/rfc5280/

[RFC5408]   G. Appenzeller, L. Martin, and M. Schertler. *Identity-Based Encryption Architecture and Supporting Data Structures.* Internet Engineering Task Force Request for Comments 5408, January 2009. https://datatracker.ietf.org/doc/rfc5408/

[RFC5409]   L. Martin and M. Schertler. *Using the Boneh-Franklin and Boneh-Boyen Identity-Based Encryption Algorithms with the Cryptographic Message Syntax (CMS).* Internet Engineering Task Force Request for Comments 5409, January 2009. https://datatracker.ietf.org/doc/rfc5409/

[RFC5750]   B. Ramsdell and S. Turner. *Secure/Multipurpose Internet Mail Extensions (S/MIME) Version 3.2 Certificate Handling.* Internet Engineering Task Force Request for Comments 5750, January 2010. https://datatracker.ietf.org/doc/rfc5750/

[RFC5751]   B. Ramsdell et. al. *Secure/Multipurpose Internet Mail Extensions (S/MIME) Version 3.2 Message Specification.* Internet Engineering Task Force Request for Comments 5751, January 2010. https://datatracker.ietf.org/doc/rfc5751/

[RFC6066]   D. Eastlake 3rd. *Transport Layer Security (TLS) Extensions: Extension Definitions.* Internet Engineering Task Force Request for Comments 6066, January 2011. https://datatracker.ietf.org/doc/rfc6066/

[RFC6698]   P. Hoffman and J. Schlyter. *The DNS-Based Authentication of Named Entities (DANE) Transport Layer Security (TLS) Protocol: TLSA.* Internet Engineering Task Force Request for Comments 6698, August 2012. https://datatracker.ietf.org/doc/rfc6698/

[RFC6960]   S. Santesson, M. Myers, R. Ankney, A. Malpani, S. Galperin and C. Adams. *X.509 Internet Public Key Infrastructure Online Certificate Status Protocol – OCSP.* Internet Engineering Task Force Request for Comments 6960, June 2013. https://datatracker.ietf.org/doc/rfc6960/

[RFC7218]   O. Gudmundsson, *Adding Acronyms to Simplify Conversations about DNS-Based Authentication of Named Entities (DANE),* Internet Engineering Task Force Request for Comments 7218, April 2014, https://datatracker.ietf.org/doc/rfc7218

[RFC7671]   V. Dukhovni, W. Hardaker, *The DNS-Based Authentication of Named Entities (DANE) Protocol: Updates and Operational Guidance.* Internet Engineering Task Force Request for Comments 7671, October 2015. https://datatracker.ietf.org/doc/rfc7671/

[RFC7672]   V. Dukhovni, W. Hardaker, *SMTP Security via Opportunistic DNS-Based Authentication of Named Entities (DANE) Transport Layer Security (TLS).* Internet Engineering Task Force Request for Comments 7672, October 2015, https://datatracker.ietf.org/doc/rfc7672/

[RFC7929]   P. Wouters. *DNS-Based Authentication of Named Entities (DANE) Bindings for OpenPGP.* Internet Engineering Task Force Request for Comments 7929, August 2016. https://datatracker.ietf.org/doc/rfc7929/

[RFC8162]   P. Hoffman, J. Schlyter. *Using Secure DNS to Associate Certificates with Domain Name for S/MIME.* Internet Engineering Task Force Request for Comments 8162, May 2017. https://datatracker.ietf.org/doc/rfc8162/

[RFC8446]   E. Rescorla. *The Transport Layer Security (TLS) Protocol Version 1.3.* Internet Engineering Task Force Request for Comments 8446, August 2018. https://datatracker.ietf.org/doc/rfc8446/

[RFC8460]   D. Margolis, A. Brotman, B. Ramakrishnan, J. Jones and M. Risher. *SMTP TLS Reporting.* Internet Engineering Task Force Request for Comments 8460, September 2018. https://datatracker.ietf.org/doc/rfc8460/

[RFC8461]   D. Margolis, B. Ramakrishnan, J. Jones and A. Brotman. SMTP MTA Strict Transport Security (MTA-STS) Internet Engineering Task Force Request for Comments 8461, September 2018. https://datatracker.ietf.org/doc/rfc8461/

B.7   Other

[BOD18-01]   Binding Operational Directive BOD-18-01 "Enhance Email and Web Security". Department of Homeland Security, October 2017. https://cyber.dhs.gov/assets/report/bod-18-01.pdf

[DOD2009]   "Digital Signatures on Email Now a DoD Requirement," Press Release, Naval Network Warfare Command, February 2, 2009.

[FPKIKRP]   Federal PKI Key Recovery Policy. Federal Public Key Infrastructure Policy Authority. Version 1.0, October 2017. https://www.idmanagement.gov/wp-content/uploads/sites/1171/uploads/fpki-krp-v1.0-10-6-2017.pdf

[GAR2005]   Simson L. Garfinkel and Robert C. Miller. 2005. Johnny 2: a user test of
               key continuity management with S/MIME and Outlook Express. In
               Proceedings of the 2005 symposium on Usable privacy and security
               (SOUPS '05). ACM, New York, NY, USA, 13-24.
               https://doi.org/10.1145/1073001.1073003

[M3AAWG]   *M3AAWG Policy Issues for Receiving Email in a World with IPv6
               Hosts.* Messaging, Malware and Mobile Anti-Abuse Working Group.
               September 2014.
               https://www.m3aawg.org/sites/default/files/document/M3AAWG_Inbou
               nd_IPv6_Policy_Issues-2014-09.pdf

[REFARCH]   *Electronic Mail (Email) Gateway Reference Architecture.* Dept. of
               Homeland Security Federal Network Resiliency Federal Interagency
               Technical Reference Architectures. DRAFT Version 1.3, June 2015.
               https://community.max.gov/display/DHS/Email+Gateway

[RFC1034]   P. Mockapetris. *DOMAIN NAMES - CONCEPTS AND FACILITIES.*
               Internet Engineering Task Force Request for Comments 1034.
               November 1987. https://datatracker.ietf.org/doc/rfc1034/

[RFC1035]   P. Mockapetris. *DOMAIN NAMES - IMPLEMENTATION AND
               SPECIFICATION.* Internet Engineering Task Force Request for
               Comments 1035. November 1987.
               https://datatracker.ietf.org/doc/rfc1035/

[RFC2505]   G. Lindberg. *Anti-Spam Recommendations for SMTP MTAs.* Internet
               Engineering Task Force Request for Comments 2505. February 1999.
               https://datatracker.ietf.org/doc/rfc2505/

[RFC4033]   R. Arends, R. Austein, M. Larson, D. Massey and S. Rose. *DNS
               Security Introduction and Requirements.* Internet Engineering Task
               Force Request for Comments 4033. March 2005.
               https://datatracker.ietf.org/doc/rfc4033/

[RFC4034]   R. Arends, et. al. *Resource Records for the DNS Security Extensions.*
               Internet Engineering Task Force Request for Comments 4034, March
               2005. https://datatracker.ietf.org/doc/rfc4034/

[RFC4035]   R. Arends, et. al. *Protocol Modifications for the DNS Security
               Extensions.* Internet Engineering Task Force Request for Comments
               4035, March 2005. https://datatracker.ietf.org/doc/rfc4035/

[RFC5782]   J. Levine. *DNS Blacklists and Whitelists.* Internet Engineering Task
               Force Request for Comments 5872, February 2010.
               https://datatracker.ietf.org/doc/rfc5782/

[RFC5322]   P. Resnick. *Internet Message Format*. Internet Engineering Task Force
                  Request for Comments 5322, October 2008.
                  https://datatracker.ietf.org/doc/rfc5322/

[RFC6186]   C. Daboo. *Use of SRV Records for Locating Email Submission/Access
                  Services*. Internet Engineering Task Force Request for Comments 6186,
                  March 2011. https://datatracker.ietf.org/doc/rfc6186/

[THREAT1]   R. Oppliger. *Secure Messaging on the Internet*. Artech House, 2014.

[THREAT2]   C. Pfleeger and S. L. Pfleeger. *Analyzing Computer Security: A
                  Threat/Vulnerability/Countermeasure Approach*. Prentice Hall, 2011.

[WHITTEN1999]   Alma Whitten and J. D. Tygar. 1999. Why Johnny can't encrypt: a
                  usability evaluation of PGP 5.0. In *Proceedings of the 8th conference on
                  USENIX Security Symposium - Volume 8* (SSYM'99), Vol. 8. USENIX
                  Association, Berkeley, CA, USA, 14-14.
                  https://www.usenix.org/conference/8th-usenix-security-
                  symposium/why-johnny-cant-encrypt-usability-evaluation-pgp-50

Appendix C—Overlay of NIST SP 800-53 Controls to Email Messaging Systems

C.1   Introduction

The following is an overlay of the NIST SP 800-53 Rev. 4 controls and gives detail on how email systems can comply with the applicable controls. This overlay partially follows the process documented in SP 800-53r4 Appendix I [SP800-53]. Here, "email system" is taken to mean any system (as defined by FIPS 199), that is said to generate, send, or store email messages for an enterprise. This section attempts to identify individual controls (or control families) that are relevant to email systems, and to select specific guidance that should be used to comply with each control.

This section does not introduce new controls that do not exist in SP 800-53 and does not declare any control unnecessary for a given system and control baseline. This section only lists controls that directly relate to deploying and operating a trustworthy email service. Further guidance is given for each control to assist administrators in meeting compliance requirements.

C.2   Applicability

The purpose of this overlay is to provide guidance for securing the various email systems used within an enterprise. This overlay has been prepared for use by federal agencies. It may be used by nongovernmental organizations on a voluntary basis.

C.3   Trustworthy Email Overlay

The overlay breaks down NIST SP 800-53 Rev. 4 controls according to specific email security protocols: Domain-based authentication (i.e., SPF, DKIM, DMARC, etc.), SMTP over TLS and end-to-end email security (i.e., S/MIME or OpenPGP). To avoid confusion as to which control applies to which technology, these controls are only listed once, with a justification included to provide more email-specific guidance as to why and how the control should apply to an email system.

Just because a control is not explicitly listed below does not mean that the control (or control family) is not applicable to an email system. Controls (or control families) that apply to all systems for a given baseline would still apply. For example, the **IA-7 CRYPTOGRAPHIC MODULE AUTHENTICATION** control could be said to apply to all systems that perform some cryptographic function for a given baseline, but administrators should already be aware of this general control, and no additional special consideration is needed just for email systems. The controls below should be seen as additional controls that should be applied for a give control baseline. A general control family may be listed below to alert administrators that there could be implications of the control family that impact email operations, so administrators should consider how the email service should address the family as applicable.

The trustworthy email service-relevant controls are listed below. The control body and relevant accompanying information is included to assist the reader, but the entire control is not included. Readers are encouraged to consult NIST SP 800-53 Rev. 4 for the full text and all accompanying material. In addition, a justification is included for each control (or control family) to state why the control is included, how it applies to email, and to provide guidance from NIST SP 800-177 (or another document) to comply with the control.

C.4   Control Baselines

The table below is taken from NIST SP 800-53 Rev. 4 Appendix D. It lists the control baselines for the three risk levels: Low, Moderate and High. To this is added the new control recommendations and extensions for the email system overlay. Additional requirements and control extensions are listed **in bold**. Justification of the additions are listed below the table.

Table C-1: Overlay Control Baselines

CONTROL Number	Control Name	CONTROL BASELINES		
		LOW	MODERATE	HIGH
Access Control (AC)				
AC-1	ACCESS CONTROL POLICY AND PROCEDURES	AC-1	AC-1	AC-1
AC-2	ACCOUNT MANAGEMENT	AC-2	AC-2 (1,2,3,4)	AC-2 (1,2,3,4, 5,11,12,13)
AC-3	ACCESS ENFORCEMENT	AC-3	AC-3	AC-3
AC-4	INFORMATION FLOW ENFORCEMENT	-	AC-4	AC-4
AC-5	SEPARATION OF DUTIES	-	AC-5	AC-5
AC-6	LEAST PRIVILEGE		AC-6 (1,2,5,9,10)	AC-6 (1,2,3,5,9, 10)
AC-7	UNSUCCESSFUL LOGON ATTEMPTS	AC-7	AC-7	AC-7
AC-8	SYSTEM USE NOTIFICATION	AC-8	AC-8	AC-8
AC-9	PREVIOUS LOGON (ACCESS) NOTIFICATION	-	-	-

AC-10	CONCURRENT SESSION CONTROL	-	-	AC-10
AC-11	DEVICE LOCK	-	AC-11(1)	AC-11(1)
AC-12	SESSION TERMINATION	-	AC-12	AC-12
AC-14	PERMITTED ACTIONS WITHOUT IDENTIFICATION OR AUTHENTICATION	AC-14	AC-14	AC-14
AC-16	SECURITY AND PRIVACY ATTRIBUTES	-	-	-
AC-17	REMOTE ACCESS	AC-17	AC-17(1,2,3,4)	AC-17(1,2,3,4)
AC-18	WIRELESS ACCESS	AC-18	AC-18 (1)	AC-18 (1,4,5)
AC-19	ACCESS CONTROL FOR MOBILE DEVICES	AC-19	AC-19 (5)	AC-19 (5)
AC-20	USE OF EXTERNAL SYSTEMS	AC-20	AC-20 (1,2)	AC-20 (1,2)
AC-21	INFORMATION SHARING	**AC-21**	**AC-21**	**AC-21**
AC-22	PUBLICALY ACCESSIBLE CONTENT	AC-22	AC-22	AC-22
AC-23	DATA MINING PROTECTION	-	-	-
AC-24	ACCESS CONTROL DECISIONS	-	-	-
AC-25	REFERENCE MONITOR	-	-	-
Awareness and Training (AT)				
AT-1	AWARENESS AND TRAINING POLICY AND PROCEDURES	AT-1	AT-1	AT-1
AT-2	AWARENESS TRAINING	**AT-2(1)**	AT-2 (1,2)	AT-2 (1,2)
AT-3	ROLE-BASED TRAINING	AT-3	AT-3	AT-3

AT-4	TRAINING RECORDS	AT-4	AT-4	AT-4
Audit and Accountability (AU)				
AU-1	AUDIT AND ACCOUNTABILITY POLICY AND PROCEDURES	AU-1	AU-1	AU-1
AU-2	AUDIT EVENTS	AU-2	AU-2 (3)	AU-2 (3)
AU-3	COUNTENT OF AUDIT RECORDS	AU-3	AU-3 (1)	AU-3 (1,2)
AU-4	AUDIT STORAGE CAPACITY	AU-4	AU-4	AU-4
AU-5	RESPONSE TO AUDIT PROCESSING FAILURES	AU-5	AU-5	AU-5 (1,2)
AU-6	AUDIT REVIEW, ANALYSIS AND REPORTING	AU-6	AU-6 (1,3)	AU-6 (1,3,5,6)
AU-7	AUDIT REDUCTION AND REPORT GENERATION	-	AU-7 (1)	AU-7 (1)
AU-8	TIME STAMPS	AU-8	AU-8 (1)	AU-8 (1)
AU-9	PROTECTION OF AUDIT INFORMATION	AU-9	AU-9 (4)	AU-9 (2,3,4)
AU-10	NON-REPUDIATION	-	-	AU-10 **(1)**
AU-11	AUDIT RECORD RETENTION	AU-11	AU-11	AU-11
AU-12	AUDIT GENERATION	AU-12	AU-12	AU-12 (1,3)
AU-13	MONITORING FOR INFORMATION DISCLOSURE	-	-	-
AU-14	SESSION AUDIT	-	-	-
AU-15	ALTERNATIVE AUDIT CAPABILITY	-	-	-
AU-16	CROSS-ORGNAZION AUDITING	-	-	-

ASSESSMENT, AUTHORIZATION AND MONITORING (CA)				
CA-1	ASSESSMENT, AUTHORIZATION AND MONITORING POLICY AND PROCEDURES	CA-1	CA-1	CA-1
CA-2	ASSESSMENTS	CA-2	CA-2 (1)	CA-2 (1,2)
CA-3	SYSTEM INTERCONNECTIONS	CA-3	CA-3 (5)	CA-3 (5)
CA-5	PLAN OF ACTION AND MILESTONES	CA-5	CA-5	CA-5
CA-6	AUTHORIZATION	CA-6	CA-6	CA-6
CA-7	CONTINUOUS MONITORING	CA-7	CA-7 (1)	CA-7 (1)
CA-8	PENETRATION TESTING	-	-	CA-8
CA-9	INTERNAL SYSTEM CONNECTIONS	CA-9	CA-9	CA-9
CONFIGURATION MANAGEMENT (CM)				
CM-1	CONFIGURATION MANAGEMENT POLICY AND PROCEDURES	CM-1	CM-1	CM-1
CM-2	BASELINE CONFIGURATION	CM-2	CM-2 (1,3,7)	CM-2 (1,2,3,7)
CM-3	CONFIGURATION CHANGE CONTROL	-	CM-3 (2)	CM-3 (1,2)
CM-4	SECURITY AND PRIVACY IMPACT ANALYSIS	CM-4	CM-4	CM-4 (1)
CM-5	ACCESS RESTRICTIONS FOR CHANGE	-	CM-5	CM-5 (1,2,3)
CM-6	CONFIGURATION SETTINGS	CM-6	CM-6	CM-6 (1,2)
CM-7	LEAST FUNCTIONALITY	CM-7	CM-7 (1,2,4)	CM-7 (1,2,5)
CM-8	SYSTEM COMPONENT INVENTORY	CM-8	CM-8 (1,3,5)	CM-8 (1,2,3,4,5)

CM-9	CONFIGURATION MANAGEMENT PLAN	-	CM-9	CM-9
CM-10	SOFTWARE USAGE RESTRICTIONS	CM-10	CM-10	CM-10
CM-11	USER-INSTALLED SOFTWARE	CM-11	CM-11	CM-11
CONTINGENCY PLANNING				
CP-1	CONTINGENCY PLANNING POLICY AND PROCEDURES	CP-1	CP-1	CP-1
CP-2	CONTINGENCY PLAN	CP-2	CP-2 (1,3,8)	CP-2 (1,2,3,4,5,8)
CP-3	CONTINGENCY TRAINING	CP-3	CP-3	CP-3 (1)
CP-4	CONTIGENCY PLAN TESTING	CP-4	CP-4(1)	CP-4 (1,2)
CP-6	ALTERNATE STORAGE SITE	-	CP-6 (1,3)	CP-6 (1,2,3)
CP-7	ALTERNATE PROCESSING SITE	-	CP-7 (1,2,3)	CP-7 (1,2,3,4)
CP-8	TELECOMMUNICATION SERVICES	-	CP-8 (1,2)	CP-8 (1,2,3,4)
CP-9	SYSTEM BACKUP	CP-9	CP-9 (1)	CP-9 (1,2,3,5)
CP-10	SYSTEM RECOVERY AND RECONSTITUION	CP-10	CP-10 (2)	CP-10 (2,4)
CP-11	ALTERNATE COMMUNICATION PROTOCOLS	-	-	-
CP-12	SAFE MODE	-	-	-
CP-13	ALTERNATIVE SECURITY MECHANISMS	-	-	-
IDENTIFICATION AND AUTHENTICATION (IA)				

IA-1	IDENTIFICATION AND AUTHENTICATION POLICY AND PROCEDURES	IA-1	IA-1	IA-1
IA-2	IDENTIFICATION AND AUTHENTICATION (ORGANIZATIONAL USERS)	IA-2(1,12)	IA-2 (1,2,3,8,11,12)	IA-2 (1,2,3,4,8,9, 11,12)
IA-3	DEVICE IDENTIFICATION AND AUTHENTICATION	-	IA-3	IA-3
IA-4	IDENTIFIER MANAGEMENT	IA-4	IA-4	IA-4
IA-5	AUTHENTICATOR MANAGEMENT	IA-5 (1,11)	IA-5 (1,2,3,11)	IA-5 (1,2,3,11)
IA-6	AUTHENTICATOR FEEDBACK	IA-6	IA-6	IA-6
IA-7	CRYPTOGRAPHIC MODUEL AUTHENTICATION	IA-7	IA-7	IA-7
IA-8	IDENTIFICATION AND AUTHENTICATION (NON-ORGANIZATIONAL USERS)	IA-8 (1,2,3,4)	IA-8 (1,2,3,4)	IA-8 (1,2,3,4)
IA-9	SERVICE IDENTIFICATION AND AUTHENTICATION	-	**IA-9 (1)**	**IA-9 (1,2)**
IA-10	ADAPTIVE IDENTIFCATION AND AUTHENTICATION	-	-	-
IA-11	RE-AUTHENTICATION	-	-	-
INCIDENT RESPONSE (IR)				
IR-1	INCIDENT RESOPNSE POLICY AND PROCEDURES	IR-1	IR-1	IR-1
IR-2	INCIDENT RESPONSE TRAINING	IR-2	IR-2	IR-2 (1,2)
IR-3	INCIDENT RESPONSE TESTING	-	IR-3 (2)	IR-3 (2)
IR-4	INCIDENT HANDLING	IR-4	IR-4 (1)	IR-4 (1,4)

IR-5	INCIDENT MONITORING	IR-5	IR-5	IR-5 (1)
IR-6	INCIDENT REPORTING	IR-6	IR-6 (1)	IR-6 (1)
IR-7	INCIDENT RESPONSE ASSISTANCE	IR-7	IR-7 (1)	IR-7 (1)
IR-8	INCIDENT RESOPNSE PLAN	IR-8	IR-8	IR-8
IR-9	INFORMATION SPILLAGE RESOPNSE	-	-	-
IR-10	INTEGRATED INFORMATION SECURITY ANALYSIS TEAM	-	-	-
MAINTENANCE (MA)				
MA-1	SYSTEM MAINTENANCE POLICY AND PROCEDURES	MA-1	MA-1	MA-1
MA-2	CONTROLLED MAINTENANCE	MA-2	MA-2	MA-2 (2)
MA-3	MAINTENANCE TOOLS	-	MA-3 (1,2)	MA-3 (1,2,3)
MA-4	NONLOCAL MAINTENANCE	MA-4	MA-4 (2)	MA-4 (2.3)
MA-5	MAINTENANCE PERSONNEL	MA-5	MA-5	MA-5 (1)
MA-6	TIMELY MAINTENANCE	-	MA-6	MA-6
MEDIA PROTECTION (MP)				
MP-1	MEDIA PROTECTION POLICY AND PROCEDURES	MP-1	MP-1	MP-1
MP-2	MEDIA ACCESS	MP-2	MP-2	MP-2
MP-3	MEDIA MARKING	-	MP-3	MP-3
MP-4	MEDIA STORAGE	-	MP-4	MP-4
MP-5	MEDIA TRANSPORT	-	MP-5 (4)	MP-5 (4)

MP-6	MEDIA SANITIZATION	MP-6	MP-6	MP-6 (1,2,3)
MP-7	MEDIA USE	MP-7	MP-7 (1)	MP-7 (1)
MP-8	MEDIA DOWNGRADING	-	-	-
PHYSICAL AND ENVIRONMENTAL PROTECTION (PE)				
PE-1	PHYSICAL AND ENVIRONMENTAL PROTECTION POLICY AND PROCEDURES	PE-1	PE-1	PE-1
PE-2	PHYSICAL ACCESS AUTHORIZATIONS	PE-2	PE-2	PE-2
PE-3	PHYSICAL ACCESS CONTROL	PE-3	PE-3	PE-3 (1)
PE-4	ACCESS CONTROL FOR TRANSMISSION	-	PE-4	PE-4
PE-5	ACCESS CONTROL FOR OUTPUT DEVICES	-	PE-5	PE-5
PE-6	MONITORING PHYSICAL ACCESS	PE-6	PE-6 (1)	PE-6 (1,4)
PE-8	VISITOR ACCESS RECORDS	PE-8	PE-8	PE-8 (1)
PE-9	POWER EQUIPMENT AND CABLING	-	PE-9	PE-9
PE-10	EMERGENCY SHUTOFF	-	PE-10	PE-10
PE-11	EMERGENCY POWER	-	PE-11	PE-11 (1)
PE-12	EMERGENCY LIGHTING	PE-12	PE-12	PE-12
PE-13	FIRE PROTECTION	PE-13	PE-13 (3)	PE-13 (1,2,3)
PE-14	TEMPERATURE AND HUMIDITY CONTROLS	PE-14	PE-14	PE-14
PE-15	WATER DAMAGE PROTECTION	PE-15	PE-15	PE-15 (1)

PE-16	DELIVERY AND REMOVAL	PE-16	PE-16	PE-16
PE-17	ALTERNATE WORK SITE	-	PE-17	PE-17
PE-18	LOCATION OF SYSTEM COMPONENTS	-	-	PE-18
PE-19	INFORMATION LEAKAGE	-	-	-
PE-20	ASSET MONITORING AND TRACKING	-	-	-
PLANNING (PL)				
PL-1	PLANNING POLICY AND PROCEDURES	PL-1	PL-1	PL-1
PL-2	SYSTEM SECURITY AND PRIVACY PLANS	PE-2	PL-2 (3)	PL-2 (3)
PL-4	RULES OF BEHAVIOR	PL-4	PL-4 (1)	PL-4 (1)
PL-7	CONCEPT OF OPERATIONS	-	-	-
PL-8	SECURITY AND PRIVACY ARCHITECTURES	-	PL-8	PL-8
PL-9	CENTRAL MANAGEMENT	-	-	-
PERSONNEL SECURITY (PS)				
PS-1	PERSONAL SECUIRTY POLICY AND PROCEDURES	PS-1	PS-1	PS-1
PS-2	POSITION RISK DESIGNATION	PS-2	PS-2	PS-2
PS-3	PERSONNEL SCREENING	PS-3	PS-3	PS-3
PS-4	PERSONNEL TERMINTATION	PS-4	PS-4	PS-4 (2)
PS-5	PERSONNEL TRANSFER	PS-5	PS-5	PS-5

PS-6	ACCESS AGREEMENTS	PS-6	PS-6	PS-6
PS-7	EXTERNAL PERSONNEL SECURITY	PS-7	PS-7	PS-7
PS-8	PERSONNEL SANCTIONS	PS-8	PS-8	PS-8
RISK ASSESSMENT (RA)				
RA-1	RISK ASSESSMENT POLICY AND PROCEDURES	RA-1	RA-1	RA-1
RA-2	SECUIRTY CATEGORIZATION	RA-2	RA-2	RA-2
RA-3	RISK ASSESSMENT	RA-3	RA-3	RA-3
RA-5	VULNERABILITY SCANNING	RA-5	RA-5 (1,2,5)	RA-5 (1,2,4,5)
RA-6	TECHNICAL SURVEILLANCE COUNTERMEASURES SURVEY	-	-	-
SYSTEM AND SERVICE ACQUISITION (SA)				
SA-1	SYSTEM AND SERVICES ACQUISITION POLICY AND PROCEDURES	SA-1	SA-1	SA-1
SA-2	ALLOCATION OF RESOURCES	SA-2	SA-2	SA-2
SA-3	SYSTEM DEVELOPMENT LIFE CYCLE	SA-3	SA-3	SA-3
SA-4	ACQUISITION PROCESS	SA-4 (10)	SA-4 (1,2,9,10)	SA-4 (1,2,9,10)
SA-5	SYSTEM DOCUMENTATION	SA-5	SA-5	SA-5
SA-8	SECURITY AND PRIVACY ENGINEERING PRINCIPLES	-	SA-8	SA-8
SA-9	EXTERNAL SYSTEM SERVICES	SA-9	SA-9 (2)	SA-9 (2)

SA-10	DEVELOPER CONFIGURATION MANAGEMENT	-	SA-10	SA-10
SA-11	DEVELOPER SECURITY TESTING AND EVALUATION	-	SA-11	SA-11
SA-12	SUPPLY CHAIN RISK MANAGEMENT	-	-	SA-12
SA-13	TRUSTWORTHINESS	-	-	-
SA-14	CRITICALITY ANALYSIS	-	-	-
SA-15	DEVELOPMENT PROCESS, STANDARDS, AND TOOLS	-	-	SA-15
SA-16	DEVELOPER-PROVIDED TRAINING	-	-	SA-16
SA-17	DEVELOPER SECURITY ARCHITECTURE AND DESIGN	-	-	SA-17
SA-18	TAMPER RESISTANCE AND DETECTION	-	-	-
SA-19	COMPONENT AUTHENTICITY	-	-	-
SA-20	CUSTOMIZED DEVELOPMENT OF CRITICAL COMPONENTS	-	-	-
SA-21	DEVELOPER SCREENING	-	-	-
SA-22	UNSUPPORTED SYSTEM COMPONENTS	-	-	-
SYSTEM AND COMMUNICATIONS PROTECTION (SC)				
SC-1	SYSTEM AND COMMUNICATIONS PROTECTION POLICY AND PROCEDURES	SC-1	SC-1	SC-1
SC-2	APPLICATION PARTITIONING	-	SC-2	SC-2
SC-3	SECURITY FUNCTION ISOLATION	-	-	SC-3

SC-4	INFORMATION IN SHARED SYSTEM RESOURCES	-	SC-4	SC-4
SC-5	DENIAL OF SERVICE PROTECTION	SC-5	SC-5	SC-5
SC-6	RESOURCE AVAILABLITY	-	-	-
SC-7	BOUNDRY PROTECTION	SC-7	SC-7 (2,3,4,7,8, **10**)	SC-7 (3,4,5,7,8, **10,11**18,21)
SC-8	TRANSMISSION CONFIDENTIALITY AND INTEGRITY	-	**SC-8 (1)**	**SC-8 (1)**
SC-10	NETWORK DISCONNECT	-	SC-10	SC-10
SC-11	TRUSTED PATH	-	-	-
SC-12	CRYPTOGRAPHIC KEY ESTABLISHMENT AND MANAGEMENT	SC-12	SC-12	SC-12 (1)
SC-13	CRYPTOGRAPHIC PROTECTION	SC-13	SC-13	SC-13
SC-15	COLLABORATIVE COMPUTING DEVICES AND APPLICATIONS	SC-15	SC-15	SC-15
SC-16	TRANSMISSION OF SECURITY AND PRIVACY ATTRIBUTES	-	-	-
SC-17	PUBLIC KEY INFRASTUCTURE CERTIFICATES	-	SC-17	SC-17
SC-18	MOBILE CODE	-	SC-18	SC-18
SC-19	VOICE OVER INTERNET PROTOCOL	-	SC-19	SC-19
SC-20	SECURE NAME/ADDRESS RESOLUTION SERVICE (AUTHORITATIVE SOURCE)	SC-20	SC-20	SC-20
SC-21	SECURE NAME/ADDRESS RESOLUTION SERVICE (RESURSIVE OR CACHING RESOLVER)	SC-21	SC-21	SC-21

SC-22	ARCHITECTURE AND PROVISIONING FOR NAME/ADDRESS RESOLUTION SERVICE	SC-22	SC-22	SC-22
SC-23	SESSION AUTHENTICITY	-	SC-23	SC-23 (5)
SC-24	FAIL IN KNOWN STATE	-	-	SC-24
SC-25	THIN NODES	-	-	-
SC-26	HONEYPOTS	-	-	-
SC-27	PLATFORM-INDEPENDENT APPLICATIONS	-	-	-
SC-28	PROTECTION OF INFORMATION AT REST	-	SC-28	SC-28
SC-29	HETEROGENEITY	-	-	-
SC-30	CONCEALMENT AND MISDIRECTION	-	-	-
SC-31	CONVERT CHANNEL ANALYSIS	-	-	-
SC-32	SYSTEM PARTITIONING	-	-	-
SC-34	NON-MODIFIABLE EXECUTABLE PROGRAMS	-	-	-
SC-35	HONEYCLIENTS	-	-	-
SC-36	DISTRIBUTED PROCESSING AND STORAGE	-	-	-
SC-37	OUT-OF-BAND CHANNELS	-	-	-
SC-38	OPERATIONS SECURITY	-	-	-
SC-39	PROCESS ISOLATION	SC-39	SC-39	SC-39
SC-40	WIRELESS LINK PROTECTION	-	-	-

SC-41	PORT AND I/O DEVICE ACCESS	-	-	-
SC-42	SENSOR CAPABILITY AND DATA	-	-	-
SC-43	USAGE RESTRICTIONS	-	-	-
SC-44	DETONATION CHAMBERS	**SC-44**	**SC-44**	**SC-44**
SYSTEM AND INFORMATION INTEGRITY (SI)				
SI-1	SYSTEM AND INFORMAITON INTEGIRTY POLICY AND PROCEDURES	SI-1	SI-1	SI-1
SI-2	FLAW REMEDIATION	SI-2	SI-2 (2)	SI-2 (1,2)
SI-3	MALICIOUS CODE PROTECTION	SI-3	SI-3 (1,2)	SI-3 (1,2)
SI-4	SYSTEM MONITORING	SI-4	SI-4 (2,4,5)	SI-4 (2,4,5)
SI-5	SECURITY ALERTS, ADVISORIES, AND DIRECTIVES	SI-5	SI-5	SI-5 (1)
SI-6	SECURITY AND PRIVACY FUNCTIONS VERIFICATION	-	-	SI-6
SI-7	SOFTWARE, FIRMWARE, AND INFORMATION INTEGRITY	-	SI-7 (1,7)	SI-7 (1,2,5,7,14)
SI-8	SPAM PROTECTION	-	SI-8 (1,2)	SI-8 (1,2)
SI-10	INFORMATION INPUT VALIDATION	-	SI-10	SI-10
SI-11	ERROR HANDLING	-	SI-11	SI-11
SI-12	INFORMATION MANAGEMENT AND RETENTION	SI-12	SI-12	SI-12
SI-13	PREDICTABLE FAILURE PREVENTION	-	-	-
SI-14	NONE-PRESISTENCE	-	-	-

SI-15	INFORMATION OUTPUT FILTERING	-	-	-
SI-16	MEMORY PROTECTION	-	SI-16	SI-16
SI-17	FAIL-SAFE PROCEDURES	-	-	-
SI-20	DE-IDENTIFICATION	-	-	-

C.5   Additional/Expanded Controls

AC-21 INFORMATION SHARING

Control:

a. Facilitate information sharing by enabling authorized users to determine whether access authorizations assigned to the sharing partner match the access restrictions and privacy authorizations on the information for [*Assignment: organization-defined information sharing circumstances where user discretion is required*]; and

b. Employ [*Assignment: organization-defined automated mechanisms or manual processes*] to assist users in making information sharing and collaboration decisions.

Justification: If an enterprise has deployed DMARC and is collecting forensic reports (see Section 4.6.5), administrators should make sure that any private data that may be contained in the report is redacted and not divulged to unauthorized parties.

AT-2 AWARENESS TRAINING

Control: Provide basic security and privacy awareness training to system users (including managers, senior executives, and contractors):

a. As part of initial training for new users;

b. When required by system changes; and

c. [*Assignment: organization-defined frequency*] thereafter.

Control Enhancements:

(1) AWARENESS TRAINING | PRACTICAL EXERCISES

The organization includes practical exercises in security awareness training that simulate actual cyber attacks.
Supplemental Guidance: Practical exercises may include, for example, no-notice social engineering attempts to collect information, gain unauthorized access, or simulate the adverse impact of opening malicious email attachments or invoking, via spear phishing attacks, malicious web links.

Justification: Administrators should have training on how to use DMARC reporting to identify and react to email borne attacks. See Section 4.6. All users of an email system should have training on how to identify and act to stop phishing attempts, opening malicious attachments and social engineering attacks using email. This could include looking for and noting the presence of digital signatures (S/MIME or OpenPGP), (see Section 5.3).

AU-10 NON-REPUDIATION

Control: The information system protects against an individual (or process acting on behalf of an individual) falsely denying having performed [*Assignment: organization-defined actions to be covered by non-repudiation*].

Control Enhancements:

(1) NON-REPUDIATION | ASSOCIATION OF IDENTIES

The information system:

(a) **Binds the identity of the information producer with the information to [*Assignment: organization-defined strength of binding*]; and**
(b) **Provides the means for authorized individuals to determine the identity of the producer of the information.**

Supplemental Guidance: This control enhancement supports audit requirements that provide organizational personnel with the means to identify who produced specific information in the event of an information transfer. Organizations determine and approve the strength of the binding between the information producer and the information based on the security category of the information and relevant risk factors

(2) NON-REPUDIATION | VALIDATE BINDING OF INFORMATION PRODUCER IDENTITY

The information system:

(a) **Validates the binding of the information producer identity to the information at [*Assignment: organization-defined frequency*]; and**
(b) **Performs [*Assignment: organization-defined actions*] in the event of a validation error.**

Supplemental Guidance: This control enhancement prevents the modification of information between production and review. The validation of bindings can be achieved, for example, by the use of cryptographic checksums. Organizations determine if validations are in response to user requests or generated automatically.

(3) NON-REPUDIATION | CHAIN OF CUSTODY

The information system maintains reviewer/releaser identity and credentials within the established chain of custody for all information reviewed or released.

Supplemental Guidance: Chain of custody is a process that tracks the movement of evidence through its collection, safeguarding, and analysis life cycle by documenting each person who handled the evidence, the date and time it was collected or transferred, and the purpose for the transfer. If the reviewer is a human or if the review function is automated but separate from the release/transfer function, the information system associates the identity of the reviewer of the information to be released with the information and the information label. In the case of human reviews, this control enhancement provides organizational officials the means to identify who reviewed and released the information. In the case of automated reviews, this control enhancement ensures that only approved review functions are employed.

(4) NON-REPUDIATION | VALIDATE BINDING OF INFORMATION REVIEWER IDENTITY

The information system:

(a) Validates the binding of the information reviewer identity to the information at the transfer or release points prior to release/transfer between [*Assignment: organization-defined security domains*]; and
(b) Performs [*Assignment: organization-defined actions*] in the event of a validation error.

Supplemental Guidance: This control enhancement prevents the modification of information between review and transfer/release. The validation of bindings can be achieved, for example, by the use of cryptographic checksums. Organizations determine validations are in response to user requests or generated automatically.

(5) (WITHDRAWN)

Supplemental Guidance:

Types of individual actions covered by non-repudiation include, for example, creating information, sending and receiving messages, approving information (e.g., indicating concurrence or signing a contract). Non-repudiation protects individuals against later claims by: (i) authors of not having authored particular documents; (ii) senders of not having transmitted messages; (iii) receivers of not having received messages; or (iv) signatories of not having signed documents. Non-repudiation services can be used to determine if information originated from a particular individual, or if an individual took specific actions (e.g., sending an email, signing a contract, approving a procurement request) or received specific information. Organizations obtain non-repudiation services by employing various techniques or mechanisms (e.g., digital signatures, digital message receipts).

Justification: Organizations using email for information transfer should use S/MIME or OpenPGP to provide authentication of the original sender (via a digital signature). In addition, the organization should provide an alternate means to publish sender digital signature certificates so that receivers can validate email digital signatures. See Section 5.3.

IA-9 SERVICE IDENTIFICATION AND AUTHENTICATION

Control: The organization identifies and authenticates [*Assignment: organization-defined information system services*] using [*Assignment: organization-defined security safeguards*].

Control Enhancements:

(1) SERVICE IDENTIFICATION AND AUTHENTICATION | INFORMATION EXCHANGE

The organization ensures that service providers receive, validate, and transmit identification and authentication information.

Justification: An organization should have certificates to authenticate MTAs that receive mail from external sources (i.e., the Internet) and for MTAs that host users' inboxes that are accessed via POP3, IMAP or Microsoft Exchange. See Section 2.3.

Control Extension:

(2) The organization should provide additional methods to validate a given MTA's certificate. Examples of this include DANE TLSA RRs (see Section 5.2.4) or SMTP Strict Transport Security (Section 5.2.5).

IP-X INDIVIDUAL PARTICIPATION (potential of entire family)

Justification: Organizations that use incoming and/or outgoing email content scanning should have a policy and set of procedures in place to make users aware of the organization's email policy. This scanning could be done for a variety of reasons (see Section 6.3.3). This includes consent, privacy notice and the remediation taken when the violations of the policy are detected.

IR-X INCIDENT RESPONSE (potential of entire family)

Justification: Organizations deploying DMARC (see Section 4.6) may need to generate a new plan to handle DMARC forensic reports that indicate their domain is being spoofed as part of a phishing campaign against a third party. This is not necessarily an attack against the organization, but an attack using the organization's reputation to subvert one or more victims. DMARC forensic reports can be used to identify these attacks that may have been unknown to the organization previously.

PS-4 PERSONNEL TERMINATION

Control: The organization, upon termination of individual employment:

a. Disables information system access within [*Assignment: organization-defined time-period*];

b. Terminates/revokes any authenticators/credentials associated with the individual;

c. Conducts exit interviews that includes discussion of [*Assignment: organization-defined information security topics*];

d. Retrieves all security-related organizational information system-related property;

e. Retains access to organizational information and information systems formerly controlled by terminated individual; and

f. Notifies [*Assignment: organization-defined personnel or roles*] within [*Assignment: organization-defined time-period*].

Justification: This control is selected so that when an email administrator leaves a position, all credentials that the administrator had access to are revoked. This includes key pairs used to with SMTP over TLS (see Section 5.2), DKIM (see Section 4.5) and/or S/MIME key pairs.

In addition, when an organization terminates a third-party email service, administrators should revoke any credentials that the third party may have had for the organizations. Examples of this include DKIM keys used by third party senders stored in the organization's DNS (see Section 4.5.11) and SPF entries used to authenticate third-party senders (see Section 4.4.4).

SC-7 BOUNDARY PROTECTION

Control: The information system:

a) Monitors and controls communications at the external boundary of the system and at key internal boundaries within the system;

b) Implements subnetworks for publicly accessible system components that are [*Selection: physically; logically*] separated from internal organizational networks; and

c) Connects to external networks or systems only through managed interfaces consisting of boundary protection devices arranged in accordance with an organizational security and privacy architecture.

Control Extensions:

(10) BOUNDARY PROTECTION | PREVENT UNAUTHORIZED EXFILTRATION

The organization prevents the unauthorized exfiltration of information across managed interfaces.

Supplemental Guidance: Safeguards implemented by organizations to prevent unauthorized exfiltration of information from information systems include, for example: (i) strict adherence to protocol formats; (ii) monitoring for beaconing from information systems; (iii) monitoring for steganography; (iv) disconnecting external network interfaces except when explicitly needed; (v) disassembling and reassembling packet headers; and (vi) employing traffic profile analysis to detect deviations from the volume/types of traffic expected within organizations or call backs to command and control centers. Devices enforcing strict adherence to protocol formats include, for example, deep packet inspection firewalls and XML gateways. These devices verify adherence to protocol formats and specification at the application layer and serve to identify vulnerabilities that cannot be detected by devices operating at the network or transport layers. This control enhancement is closely associated with cross-domain solutions and system guards enforcing information flow requirements.

(11) BOUNDARY PROTECTION | RESTRICT INCOMING COMMUNICATIONS TRAFFIC

The information system only allows incoming communications from [*Assignment: organization-defined authorized sources*] to be routed to [*Assignment: organization-defined authorized destinations*].

Supplemental Guidance: This control enhancement provides determinations that source and destination address pairs represent authorized/allowed communications. Such determinations can be based on several factors including, for example, the presence of such address pairs in the lists of authorized/allowed communications; the absence of such address pairs in lists of unauthorized/disallowed pairs; or meeting more general rules for authorized/allowed source and destination pairs.

Justification: Email systems should have incoming mail filters to detect, quarantine or reject mail from known bad senders (e.g., known Spam or malicious senders). Email systems should also implement outgoing mail filters to prevent sensitive data exfiltration and detect internal hosts that may be compromised to send Spam using the organization's reputation to spoof victims.

SC-8 TRANSMISSION CONFIDENTIALITY AND INTEGRITY

Control: The information system protects the [*Selection (one or more): confidentiality; integrity*] of transmitted information.

Control Enhancements:

(1) TRANSMISSION CONFIDENTIALITY AND INTEGRITY | CRYPTOGRAPHIC OR ALTERNATE PHYSICAL PROTECTION

The information system implements cryptographic mechanisms to [*Selection (one or more): prevent unauthorized disclosure of information; detect changes to information*] during transmission unless otherwise protected by [*Assignment: organization-defined alternative physical safeguards*].

Supplemental Guidance: Encrypting information for transmission protects information from unauthorized disclosure and modification. Cryptographic mechanisms implemented to protect information integrity include, for example, cryptographic hash functions which have common application in digital signatures, checksums, and message authentication codes. Alternative physical security safeguards include, for example, protected distribution systems.

Justification: Email systems should deploy security protocols to protect the integrity of email messages and the confidentially of messages in transit. For integrity protection, email systems should use DKIM (see Section 4.5) and/or S/MIME digital signatures (see Section 5.3) when sending messages. For confidentiality, email systems should use SMTP over TLS (see Section 5.2).

SC-23 SESSION AUTHENTICITY

Control: The information system protects the authenticity of communications sessions.

Supplemental Guidance: This control addresses communications protection at the session, versus packet level (e.g., sessions in service-oriented architectures providing web-based services) and establishes grounds for confidence at both ends of communications sessions in ongoing identities of other parties and in the validity of information transmitted. Authenticity protection includes, for example, protecting against man-in-the-middle attacks/session hijacking and the insertion of false information into sessions.

Control Enhancements:

(5) SESSION AUTHENTICITY | ALLOWED CERTIFICATE AUTHORITIES

The information system only allows the use of [*Assignment: organization-defined certificate authorities*] for verification of the establishment of protected sessions.

Supplemental Guidance: Reliance on certificate authorities (CAs) for the establishment of secure sessions includes, for example, the use of Secure Socket Layer (SSL) and/or Transport Layer Security (TLS) certificates. These certificates, after verification by their respective CAs, facilitate the establishment of protected sessions between web clients and web servers.

Justification: Prior to establishing a TLS connection for SMTP transmission of email, a sending MTA should authenticate the certificate provided by the receiving MTA. This authentication could be PKIX, or an alternative method (e.g., DANE, SMTP-STS, etc.). See Section 5.2 for details.

SC-44 DETONATION CHAMBERS

Control: The organization employs a detonation chamber capability within [*Assignment: organization-defined system, system component, or location*].

Supplemental Guidance: Detonation chambers, also known as dynamic execution environments, allow organizations to open email attachments, execute untrusted or suspicious applications, and execute Universal Resource Locator (URL) requests in the safety of an isolated environment or a virtualized sandbox. These protected and isolated execution environments provide a means of determining whether the associated attachments or applications contain malicious code. While related to the concept of deception nets, this control is not intended to maintain a long-term environment in which adversaries can operate and their actions can be observed. Rather, it is intended to quickly identify malicious code and reduce the likelihood that the code is propagated to user environments of operation (or prevent such propagation completely).

Justification: Incoming email and attachments from outside sources should be examined in detonation chambers to protect against malicious code or URLs contained in the email message. See Section 6.